RAGNAR'S URBAN SURVIVAL

A Hard-Times Guide to Staying Alive in the City

Ragnar Benson

PALADIN PRESS • BOULDER, COLORADO

Also by Ragnar Benson
Acquiring New ID
Bull's-Eye: Crossbows
Do-It-Yourself Medicine
Eating Cheap
Hardcore Poaching
Live Off the Land in the City and Country
Mantrapping
Modern Survival Retreat
Modern Weapons Caching
The Most Dangerous Game: Advanced Mantrapping Techniques
Ragnar's Action Encyclopedia, Volumes 1 and 2
Ragnar's Guide to the Underground Economy
Ragnar's Ten Best Traps . . . And a Few Others That Are Damn Good, Too
Survival Poaching
Survivalist's Medicine Chest
The Survival Retreat: A Total Plan for Retreat Defense
Switchblade: The Ace of Blades

Ragnar's Urban Survival:
A Hard-Times Guide to Staying Alive in the City
by Ragnar Benson

Copyright © 2000 by Ragnar Benson

ISBN 1-58160-059-3
Printed in the United States of America

Published by Paladin Press, a division of
Paladin Enterprises, Inc., P.O. Box 1307,
Boulder, Colorado 80306, USA.
(303) 443-7250

Direct inquiries and/or orders to the above address.

PALADIN, PALADIN PRESS, and the "horse head" design
are trademarks belonging to Paladin Enterprises and
registered in United States Patent and Trademark Office.

All rights reserved. Except for use in a review, no
portion of this book may be reproduced in any form
without the express written permission of the publisher.

Neither the author nor the publisher assumes
any responsibility for the use or misuse of
information contained in this book.

Visit our Web site at www.paladin-press.com

Table of Contents

Introduction	1
Chapter 1: Basic Survival Philosophy	7
Chapter 2: Combat in Built-Up Areas	19
Chapter 3: The Government's View of Survivalists	29
Chapter 4: Water	37
Chapter 5: Sources of Energy	55
Chapter 6: Food	73
Chapter 7: Survival Food Preparation	99
Chapter 8: Emergency Shelter in Cities	119
Chapter 9: Caching and Storage	131
Chapter 10: Trading	143
Chapter 11: Guns	157
Chapter 12: Survival Nursing	173
Conclusion	185
About the Author	191

Warning

Technical data presented here, particularly data on ammunition and on the use, adjustment, and alteration of firearms, inevitably reflect the author's individual beliefs and experiences with particular firearms, equipment, and components under specific circumstances that the reader cannot duplicate exactly. The information in this book should therefore be used for guidance only and approached with great caution. Neither the author, publisher, nor distributors assume any responsibility for the use or misuse of information contained in this book.

Preface

I am frequently asked if city survival is similar to survival in the country or wilderness. Answering that question is a major premise of this book. Since what many people consider wilderness survival actually refers to recreational activities—frequently practiced by elitist yuppies in SUVs— we must set these practices aside before we can answer the question: Is city survival different from rural survival?

The short answer is that city survival is very much like rural survival, only different. It is identical in that the same basic Rule of Threes applies in either place, and that the Rule of Survival Thermodynamics also is still in force. (You'll learn about these rules soon.) None of these basics has been repealed.

We also know that caching and storage remain cornerstones of any

A great many cities have been the scene of vicious battles already in the 20th century. It is foolish not to plan for such in the 21st century.

survival program. The same is true of the rule about avoiding falling into refugee status.

Hunting and gathering skills are still necessary in the city, however, these skills will be adapted to the city environment. Renewable sources of food can be established, but again, they will be much different from their rural counterparts.

Shelter is perhaps initially easier to find in the city, but the dangers of theft, bullying, and depredation will be much greater. Understanding the need for secrecy while living among large numbers of people is very important.

Rural survivalists can, in my opinion, make do without guns. Some notable 20th century survivors, such as Bill Moreland—who survived alone for 13 years in Idaho's rugged Clearwater National Forest—did without guns for an extended period of years. In the city it's an entirely different matter. Not only are firearms vital, at least some must be silenced. We had better know how to make and deploy effective silencers.

As a boy in post-World War I Germany, my father walked 3 miles per day carrying two 25-liter (approximately 5 gallon) cans to the river and back. There was a group of revolutionary German soldiers continually trying to shoot anyone—especially kids—out on the street; the reason why is lost in history. Logic suggests that poison gas from incessant warfare continually swirling around them would have poisoned the water, but no one died from the water. Finding potable water in a city survival situation can be an incredible problem. Without advance preparation, the situation could be terminal.

With a shortage of water, irrigating a garden will be a challenge and may violate the Rule of Survival Thermodynamics. But city gardens are still possible. They are being raised successfully even as I write, although they are too often of an ornamental or hobby nature.

City survivors frequently neglect planning for caching and food storage till it is too late. Raised, or perhaps more accurately, managed, livestock as a renewable source of food is also possible. These activities are not intuitive, and those who try to learn after the flag goes up will become casualties.

What about energy in the city? It's required to cook, preserve food, heat, and provide light. It's necessary for travel and communications, as well. City survivors have more options regarding energy, but these must entail extremely clever procurement and deployment strategies—much more so than in rural situations. My experts who have been there and done that will speak to this issue.

Food in the city, no matter how it's procured, arrives in a great rush. At harvest time, fruits and vegaetables must be quickly dealt with before they spoil. Where livestock is available, city dwellers will need to learn all the survival tricks of slaughtering, butchering, storing, and preserving meat.

One thing that will be dramatically different for people used to city life is the extent to which survivors *must* band together for mutual protection and specialization. Voluntary specialization is a characteristic of any free, successful economy. For everyone's benefit, people must be free to do whatever they do best and to trade for their best price. Without these mechanisms, the wrong goods are produced in the wrong quantity and quality. Survivors, unskilled in certain areas, are forced to spend precious hours doing for themselves what other, more skilled people could do better, quicker, and cheaper for them. Every society moves to specialization, either under the table or on the table. Unless specialization occurs fairly quickly, there won't be enough hours in the day to get everything done. Survival is not an activity for the lazy.

Resourceful, learned scrounging has always played a major role in any city survival program. We need to think about these skills now.

In this volume I will share what I've learned about surviving in the city—that is my commitment to readers. Because as many others have learned the hard way, the need for these skills can occur with lightning-like suddenness.

—Ragnar Benson

Introduction

Open space between our cities seems to be disappearing, often with a puzzling intensity and speed. What was just a few short years ago raw countryside filled with idyllic little farms, quaint, remote villages, and gravel roads has been developed into government office complexes, apartment complexes, cinema complexes, and parking complexes.

As young men growing up on the farm, we understood that we made up the 12 percent of the nation's citizens who provided the rest of the country's food and fiber. Eighty-acre family farms were not only common, but—much more surprising—economically viable. Ours was a most humble existence, but it provided sufficient goods on which to live.

Then farm efficiency increased, decreasing what we spent on food, and we farmers diminished to 4 percent of the population. There was a hue and cry throughout the land to save the family farm. Speaking personally, I do not know if we really wanted to be saved to the down-and-dirty existence small-farm life provides when our brothers and sisters could more easily go to town and prosper. In any event, the vast majority of us could not put the necessary capital and expertise together required to continue to farm in a modern environment.

Currently, I am informed, less than 2 percent still till the nation's soil. Farm field and demonstration days I still attend reflect this situation. They are a mere shadow of former times.

Our military recognizes this widening urban development. FM 90-10-1: An Infantryman's Guide to Urban Combat points out that in the past 20 years, cities have spread dramatically. They are "losing their previously well-defined boundaries and are extending into the countryside. Highways, canals, and railroads have been built to connect population centers."

Even rural areas that manage to retain some of their farm village-like character are now interconnected by vast networks of all-weather secondary roads. This is a bureaucratic way of saying that even if an area looks like a rural farm community, we can quickly turn it into a tank park when the need arises.

Contending governments maneuvering opposing armies historically selected wide-open areas in which to operate, but the 20th

The era of the family farm has passed.

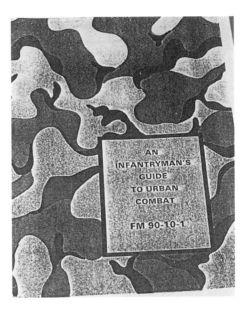

FM 90-10-1: An Infantryman's Guide to Urban Combat contains an analysis of the modern landscape.

INTRODUCTION

Cities are viewed by modern militaries as having three terrain features—underground, grade level, and high-rise—similar to those of open country.

More of us are living in built-up areas characterized by row upon row of apartments.

century has already proved to be the century of city conflict. Major battles are fought in cities now, not out in open country.

Cities are perceived to be vital because they are the places of politics, propaganda, transportation, storage, commerce and industry, and culture. Soviet Field Marshal Georgi Zhukov, for instance, had no illusions regarding the strategic value of Berlin at the conclusion of World War II. Militarily, Berlin had little actual value; but from a propaganda standpoint Berlin was vital. Instead of retreating to the more easily defended south of Germany, the Nazis were sucked into this Soviet subterfuge, defending the city down to the last plane, tank, and Hitler Youth member.

At least 34 major battles have been fought in large metropolitan areas during the past 100 years. It's a long list, including such notable places as Madrid (if you don't understand the Spanish

Civil War, no war in the 20th century can be understood), Warsaw (the unbelievably horrible Warsaw Ghetto comes to mind), Seoul (four times trounced in the brief Korean War), Saigon (symbolically drawing the curtain on U.S. involvement in southeast Asia), and Beirut (from which much information for this manual is drawn).

Rather than on farms, we will be living in housing complexes when crises hit.

We tend to think of guerrilla warfare as being a product of the countryside, as with Maj. Gen. Orde Wingate's Chindits, who operated in northern Burma during World War II, or Mao's and Stalin's statements that counterrevolutions start on the farm.

This is not true today. Wise military people prepare to fight the next war, not to refight the last. Today our military trains to fight urban guerrillas in built-up areas.

This volume does not directly relate to urban warfare. It does recognize the truth that most of us will likely live in cities, because cities are mostly what there are now. The volume also fully recognizes the survival truth that refugees are never survivors. In its most modern interpretation, survival is living free of government control. Refugees certainly do not fit this definition, probably explaining why they die in such large numbers.

Because contending governments like to fight in cities and because it would be folly to leave our familiar places in cities, we must learn to survive in cities. Like the romantic image of great, sweeping cavalry charges run across grass-carpeted rolling hills, we must face the fact that rural survival is something of a nostalgic notion. Even if wilderness survival was ever really a practical device, it isn't viable today. We don't live in rural areas, and rural areas are not where battles will be fought.

Lightning-fast surprise attacks determined to seize enemy urban strongpoints are a cornerstone of warfare in built-up places. Simply

INTRODUCTION 5

Those who rely on the government will probably end up dead.

put, we could instantly find ourselves engulfed in an urban conflict, neither of our choosing nor of our doing. Such an action would instantly require deployment of survival supplies and superb survival skills. This is perhaps more true in Europe and Asia, but this world is a shrinking place.

As a direct result of the 20th century's being the century of urban warfare and survival, we have a tremendous body of experts who have learned how to live off the land in the city. "Been there, done that" is their motto.

Ranging from my father, who survived World War I in Kassel, Germany, to the many Lebanese exchange students currently attending our land grant colleges, there are experts to call on. Many grew up believing there was no other way of life.

When starting this volume, I vividly recalled the comments made by a senior editor of a large magazine chain that, ironically, included a survival magazine. Force of habit, custom, family, and job-related issues kept her in New York City. Admittedly, it's one of the world's truly tough places to survive under even good circumstances.

"When the flag goes up," she very seriously explained, "people like me are all going to die. People in the country will live, but I have no chance."

This is not true. We now know with certainty that residents of Beirut, Berlin, and Madrid survived in great numbers under absolutely brutal conditions. They did not have the benefit of prior experience, a survival philosophy, or any special advance preparation. We can have all these in place, as the reader will quickly discover.

Chapter 1

Basic Survival Philosophy

"When it is extremely important that your pants stay up, use both a belt and suspenders, along with buttons on your shirttails," a Russian proverb says. This basic homily echoes the Golden Rule of Survival, known as the Rule of Threes.

The Pacific Northwest Nez Percé Indians probably deserve the most thanks for refining this rule into a genuinely workable survival plan. Most likely this plan became part of their culture in about 1730 with arrival of their first horses. The Nez Percé were the only tribe of North American Indians who learned to selectively breed their stock, leading to development of the famous Appaloosa warhorse.

The Nez Percé were unique in several other regards. They were the only tribe that did not routinely starve every winter. They had a lifesaving survival plan that soon became an integral part of their culture.

It was a model of simplicity, explaining in large part its great success. The Nez Percé discovered that for everything really, truly important to life, three separate and distinct methods of supply must be developed. As it evolved through the years, this Rule of Threes proved to be extremely wise. Obviously the Nez Percé applied this rule to their life in the country, but experienced city survivors have found that it works equally well for them.

The system's corollary proved equally profound. The Nez Percé found—especially in the short run—it does not take very much in an absolute sense to stay alive. Elements of basic survival were simply seen as food, water, energy, shelter, and possibly articles of personal encouragement. In our culture these personal items might be art, music, or perhaps a Bible. One woman I know believes this should include a hot shower once a week. Because these items are so absolutely necessary, positive provision for their supply must be made. Twentieth-century experience suggests that we must include medications, clothing, and self-defense in this list. But we also now know passive defense systems— such as simply laying low and hiding—are often as effective as active ones.

Nez Percé Indians lived well as a result of their survival philosophy.

First contact with Europeans for the Nez Percé came on September 20, 1805, when Lewis and Clark rode down out of the mountains into their remote area of what is now the state of Idaho. At that time the Nez Percé already owned six modern (for that era) rifles! These had been bartered from the Mandans and Hidatsa, who had bought them from French and British traders. Because their Appaloosa horses were so valuable, the Nez Percé were able to trade for equally valuable items such as rifles, powder, and balls. Another rule of survival comes into view.

Even before firearms, the Nez Percé were able to survive using their Rule of Threes. Later on, having a few figurative trade dollars in their pouches allowed them to survive in much better style. It's still true today—those with their financial houses in order will survive better and more easily than those who are forced to live under more basic conditions. Those with money for guns and ammo, especially in cities, have a far better chance at survival.

While the basic Rule of Threes works in a day-to-day, practical sense in the city or country, it can also be deployed by those who are into recreational nuts-twigs-and-berries primitive survival. The rule gently draws all of us into a workable plan. People don't have to leave their current homes for mice-infested, drafty cabins in the hills in order to live.

FOOD

Employing the Rule of Threes, we know that when food is vital for you and your family's survival, you should develop at least three separate and distinct sources of supply. No one source can in any way be dependent on the other for its implementation. Each on its own should be capable of feeding you and your family during an emergency.

My father and his family in post-World War I Germany, for example, relied on the rabbits and pigeons they tended, the garden vegetables they raised, and wild edibles they found in the fields and city parks, as well as what they bartered for with surrounding farmers. They lived in the center of a large city.

In a more modern context, city dwellers can expect to rely on their domestic rabbits, their gardens, and scrounged edibles gathered from surrounding fields, parks, and rivers, as well as consumption of stocks of previously stored supplies as needed.

The other vital rule is the Rule of Survival Thermodynamics. This means that you must never put more energy into a survival activity than is taken out. Those who fail to heed this warning quickly become casualties.

This generally rules out sport hunting and fishing, but opportunistic shooting of critters for the pot in the course of other survival-related activities probably would not violate this precept.

Survivors who have adequately prepared can expect to go to the food shelf to resupply.

Rabbits are ideal food animals for city survivors. They eat virtually anything green and are extremely prolific.

Keep in mind that in Indian cultures, most edible critters were caught in snares or deadfalls. Theories of fair chase and conservation did not enter the equation.

Gardening as a survival technique may also be impractical for many people who haven't gardened before in their specific area. However, survivors who are already practiced in their city-based gardening skills can probably see a net gain for their efforts.

Foraging in the city can also yield food, but it is difficult. Our early Indians learned to properly treat acorn meat (washing out the tannic acid), hunt wild bees, dig edible flower bulbs, and collect cattails and many other edible plants. Today, in the city or country, the only foraging technique that practically qualifies for most Americans involves gathering cattails. Other edibles are sparse, hard to recognize, of little food value, and generally unavailable in winter. As a practical matter, collecting nuts, berries, and twigs generally makes little survival sense.

But the good news for city dwellers is that cattails are every-

BASIC SURVIVAL PHILOSOPHY

Even when very large game is targeted, sport fishing and hunting is not usually viable for survivors.

Only opportunistic game shooting done while undertaking other jobs is a viable survival technique.

where. My old, old account regarding cattails with which many survivors are already familiar, involves the time I was riding in a taxi from National Airport at Washington, D.C., (now Ronald Reagan National Airport) into town with a skeptical newspaper reporter anxious to discredit all survivors. We passed acre upon acre of cattails growing wild along the Potomac River. My point about these being an excellent survival food that was commonly available in an emergency was instantly made.

During the fall and winter, cattail roots can be sliced and boiled, substituting for potatoes. In spring and summer, tender shoots can be harvested and steamed for the table. In season, cattail pollen is relatively easy to collect, substituting for flour as much as 50 percent by volume in biscuits. Green cattail flowers are also nutritious and abundant when collected and eaten before they mature and brown. Most important, easily identified cattails grow everywhere in the United States in great abundance. Nothing else looks like a cattail and they are never toxic. The danger is, of course, that over time, many city survivors will obliterate limited city cattail beds, but so far this has not happened. Despite my best efforts at promotion, few people seem to know about and use cattails!

Another valuable food source available to city dwellers is rabbits and pigeons. Those who have never raised livestock before will find these animals fairly easy to raise. Rabbits are some of the best composters available, and they eat just about any cellulose at hand. After learning how to handle them, three females and a buck will produce enough meat for two rabbit-meat meals per week, while simultaneously fertilizing the garden. And they are good city animals. I recently discovered an extensive, mostly hidden, rabbit enterprise in a crowded English city.

Cattails grow next to a housing development. This vegetable does not pick up surrounding pollution and, when well cleaned, is always safe and nutritious.

Members of this family raising rabbits in the heart of a large industrial English city are practicing survival skills and don't even know it.

As a food source, common pigeons are another critter with great charm when raised in the city. They fly out to get their own food and water from a roost that can be established virtually anywhere. Fifteen adults easily produce sufficient meat for another two meals per week. There will be more about raising these critters in the city in subsequent chapters.

Game animals of all kinds from rabbits to carp are best

BASIC SURVIVAL PHILOSOPHY

Survivors in a life-and-death setting must trap all of their game. Sport hunting and fishing risks using more calories than are earned.

Getting raw grain from farmers may not be practical or possible for city survivors.

Grain terminals, if they can be reached, have sufficient food for a city for a year. Fresh water is a plus.

trapped. Learning how isn't difficult. Set out great numbers of traps, repeating what works. In cities, expect to catch cats, dogs, and rats; in the country, look for deer, rabbits, and geese. Trapping wild or semi-wild game is part of the Rule of Threes for both city and rural survival.

Bartering with farmers and stockmen for edibles is another alternative. Those living near farms may be able learn how to preserve harvests themselves. Like country survivors, the city variety must be willing and able to preserve their own food.

CACHING AND STORING

Most city survivors will elect to make stockpiling a large part of their three-legged food survival program. Understanding how to effectively stockpile intimidates some folks. Here's a simple way to determine what you'll need: Instead of guessing about what you think

Plastic barrels can be used for deep, long-term hiding and caching of survival supplies.

you'll need, just start buying doubles of all the essential items you normally purchase. For 8 months preceding the hour of need, start saving all these extra supplies in one set-aside survival area. Soon there will be more than enough lightbulbs, hand soap, sanitary napkins, coffee, and so on, to see you past an emergency.

WATER

Three sources of potable water are a must. One source could be the municipal pipe into your home, but is not a source you can count on. City dwellers might consider renting a shallow well auger to sink their own backyard well. It is not too early to think about the availability of pond, river, or lake water as part of one's water Rule of Threes. You'll also want to consider a rig to catch and store rainwater from house and building roofs. All that is needed to implement this collection storage plan in most city circumstances are some extra gutter, plastic tarp, and plastic storage barrels (which for some reason are most often blue). Other suggestions are

BASIC SURVIVAL PHILOSOPHY

to store water in bottles, bladders such as waterbeds, or fiberglass water tanks.

ENERGY

Planning three sources of energy is not tough once you overcome the realization that they probably all must be purchased well ahead of need or, within cities, actively scrounged up by creative survivors. I plan to use 1,000 gallons of stored fuel oil to run my generator and provide some heat, and 1,000 gallons of propane to cook, heat water, and perhaps warm the house. Large propane storage tanks may not be legal in cities, but I know of two current survivors who have 1,000-gallon propane tanks buried out of sight under their garage floor. My third energy source is 25 cords of scrap wood that I can replenish from abandoned buildings and storage areas as needed. I could heat, cook, and survive with scrap pallet wood alone.

Depending on one's specific circumstances, there are also coal, geothermal devices, solar cells, and fuel cells. Small, increasingly inexpensive fuel cells used for direct electrical conversion from LP (liquid propane) gas are coming on the scene. There are also very unconventional fuel sources. My father ran out every time a team of horses came by to scoop up any road apples, which were either dried for fuel or shoveled into the garden as fertilizer. Although road apples have gone the way of dinosaurs in most places, your city survival plan will eventually entail these sorts of improvisations.

SHELTER

Shelter in our list of threes also encompasses clothing and emergency medical supplies. Most people in our outdoor-oriented society have sufficient boots, jackets, and warm, woolly sweaters to wear when the place can't be kept at 62 degrees. Emergency medical supplies are a complex, separate, and very philosophical issue that should be addressed by survivors as quickly as possible.

Shelter might be your present home or apartment. First backup can include an abandoned cellar, backyard dugout, a tent, or perhaps a cooperative area, depending on risk levels. Others may have a travel camper, old bus body, or even an old warehouse in which to hide a shelter. You may make tentative plans to move in with your kids or back to your parents. Anything just so long as the Rule of Threes relative to shelters is addressed.

It's tough advice for city people, but no matter what, never, never become a refugee. Survival rates among refugees with no control of their destinies are dismal. Refugees are totally the wards of government. If you believe the government does an adequate job of running the post office, Social Security, and the military, then you will probably be satisfied with the way it will run your life as a refugee. Effective hiding is an important part of city survival as it relates to the Rule of Threes.

Our technology is changing quickly. For this and reasons of

Russian survivors also postulated the Rule of Threes, but it didn't maintain their Soviet Union.

A Russian flag flies over the old Soviet embassy in Bangkok. Russians' use of the Rule of Threes often covers only social situations, e.g.: If you want your flag pole to stay up, set it in concrete and use double-strength metal pipe and guy wires.

BASIC SURVIVAL PHILOSOPHY

personal circumstances, skills, and likes and dislikes, our personal survival plans are never final. Readers should include survival means that I have never dreamed of within their own Rule of Threes. A survivor in east Boise, Idaho, has his own private geothermal heat well, for instance! We will miss opportunities unless we are constantly alert for them.

This is the overall guiding philosophy to survival. Obviously it applies to city survival. Commit to it and you will live. To gloss over parts of it is to suffer extreme consequences.

Chapter 2

Combat in Built-Up Areas

Warfare once took part largely over natural terrain, including mountaintops, rolling hills, jungles, and barriers such as rivers and lakes. However, most battles are now fought on urban terrain, which consists mostly of man-made features. Chiefly, these are tall buildings, rows of solidly built, difficult-to-breach concrete factory buildings, rows of flammable dwellings two stories high or less, wide open four-lane highways leading to places commanders don't necessarily wish their infantry to go, and elaborate sewer and subway systems.

In the eyes of the military leader, city buildings provide cover and concealment to the enemy, block potential fields of fire, limit observation, and severely limit use of armor and artillery forces, which cannot elevate or depress their guns sufficiently to reach many targets. As a practical matter, only high-angle mortars are thought to be effective in city terrain, and even then three to five times as many of them are required.

Many buildings will be reduced to rubble in the course of urban combat.

19

In spite of this great disadvantage, arrogant commanders often order their troops and armor into cities when encirclement—trapping defenders in a city—might possibly be a wiser tactic. Cities have grown so large and of such strategic importance that commanders no longer have the advantage of starving them out, many experts claim. Grozniy in Chechnya is a good, fairly recent example; rebels there got more than 100 Russian armored vehicles before it was over. But, nevertheless, we often wonder at the bravado with which generals sacrifice their men and equipment engaging in city warfare.

Tall, imposing buildings will become like major high hills dominating an urban area. Commanders will likely use these for gun positions.

The end result for city survivors is about the same. Either they must avoid hostile attackers, or their own defenders might become hostile and create as many problems as the attacking infantry.

The North Vietnamese tunnel system and our tunnel rats got a lot of publicity, but starting as early as the Spanish Civil War (1936-1939) defenders actively used underground workings to either infiltrate or exfiltrate cities. Some people estimate that the defenders of the Warsaw Ghetto could have held out against the Nazis as many as 30 additional days by clever use of Warsaw's extensive sewer system.

Underground works are currently one of the first places attacking soldiers attempt to secure. Unless completely walled off and cleverly camouflaged, interconnecting sewer works and utility tunnels are not places of choice for city survivors to take refuge. Modern urban soldiers with good leadership no longer make uninformed snap decisions regarding underground terrain. Reportedly, survey maps of the world's major cities underground are part of our covert military information-gathering process. Saddam may be

COMBAT IN BUILT-UP AREAS 21

Communications and helicopters will be important within contested cities, but their usefulness will be limited by the nature of the terrain.

rightfully paranoid about our efforts to find out about Baghdad's sewers.

City warfare is similar to warfare in the country in many regards. Modern, properly led infantry elements preparing to take a hill no longer line up at the base to receive a pep talk from their leaders, listen to martial bagpipe music, and then charge on up. Instead, a huge bomb is probably dropped on top of the hill and the infantry instantly helicoptered in for an assault from the top down. Urban combat is envisioned as being only slightly different.

Commanders will identify the tallest, most impressive high-rise building in the center of a contested city—one that is sufficiently stout to support rocket launchers, heavy machine guns, and mortars. Incredibly, modern urban warfare doctrine suggests that these prominent buildings should be taken by helicopter assault groups moving from the top down, often after high explosives placed on the top floors clear them of defenders.

When enemy fire and other considerations preclude helicopters, it is the current wisdom that attacking infantry forces first climb to the top of targeted buildings on fire escapes or inside stairs. Once on top, they begin their assault, fighting their way back down again. Defenders will no doubt attempt to hinder these assaults by placing barbed wire, antipersonnel mines, and other obstacles in stairwells to impede the progress of attacking forces.

Out in the country, high-profile hills are not good places to survive. The same is true in cities. The tallest buildings will likely be at the center of heavy fighting. Survivors should avoid these.

Radio communications between soldiers and commanders in cities are often poor, resulting in both good and bad conditions for city survivors—a soldier on his own may be easier to deal with, but on the other hand he is also unencumbered by his commander's ethical directives.

Incredibly, commercial phone systems—most of which operate through deeply buried conduit-encased lines—are seen as being more resistant to attack. Contending parties will each attempt to appropriate civilian phone service for their own use. Survivors near central telephone switch facilities may be subject to some rude treatment.

Arrogant, inexperienced urban commanders often send their armor into situations where it cannot maneuver and is subsequently destroyed by defending citizens.

Groups of attacking infantry, as well as defenders, will quickly be splintered into small, isolated units, operating completely independently. Each will be responsible for its own decisions, many of which may not be wise or—at a minimum—may not fit into the big picture. The

Small, individual actions fought with great intensity characterize urban combat.

loss of a small group of infantry many not be immediately obvious. Exactly why it was lost, under what specific circumstances, may never ever come to light.

This brings us to realize that often within cities under attack, small groups of isolated infantry may possibly be taken out with no repercussions for the survivors. But the probability is that one never knows when this will be true: Battlefield communications capabilities are increasing dramatically. It is best not to count on this defense when other devices such as deep hiding are available.

City survivors who very cleverly hide their presence in unobtrusive, untargeted places often survive nicely. This will probably entail removing all signs of their retreat. They will have to learn the art of camouflaging and carefully hide all survival supplies—all

COMBAT IN BUILT-UP AREAS 23

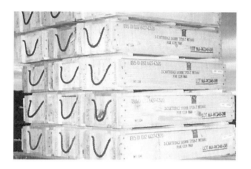

Huge quantities of supplies will disappear during any urban combat situation. Survivors with their limited resources should think carefully before committing themselves to urban combat.

signs of their presence—while simultaneously not participating in the war raging about them.

This is not easy. City survivors report that because of crowded living conditions, accompanied by great sanitary and disposal problems, retreats are frequently located by smell alone! Even cooking food among the smell of destruction can be an instant giveaway.

Military targets in cities, when they are exposed, are most frequently visible at ranges of 100 meters or less. As a result, urban conflict tends to be low-tech. Infantry units will have to have some compelling reason to come into your immediate area; otherwise, your retreat may be completely overlooked.

Close, violent combat with light auto and semiauto weapons, flamethrowers, hand grenades, mines, and light antitank weapons (taking the place of artillery), is common in urban warfare. Obviously, many traditionally civilian weapons likely to be in the hands of urban survivors will work nicely in these situations. Defenders will not have to rely on standard military equipment to make an adequate showing. Knowing that the reliable, scope-sighted semiauto .22-caliber rifle could be used at the short ranges in cities to trump well-armed attackers is certainly a source of comfort.

Urban conflict is notorious for the vast, virtually disproportionate amount of munitions it chews up. Internal defenders without regular lines of resupply are at an advantage if they have enough prepositioned supplies. Theft of war materiel is a great concern for attacking forces, but since capturing enemy supplies is risky, experienced city fighters report that most of their stuff came from pre-existing, internal stockpiles. Again, city survivors should only get involved if their most immediate area is compromised.

The rule of thumb in this case is that, again, city survivors should not get involved in battles. If they do, their precious private supplies will be quickly exhausted. Replacement by capture does not work and should not be part of a survival plan, experts claim.

This advice proved accurate in the reduction of Berlin and Beirut, but not so accurate in the Warsaw Ghetto. Certainly it's a matter of

Modern cities have grown together, producing situations in which the military commanders will send their troops and equipment through buildings rather than down streets.

how badly either side wants to continue to fight and what sorts of skilled manpower are available.

City combat is different from combat in the countryside in some deadly regards. A veteran of World War II city fighting recalls that whenever a city had to be taken, he and his fellow soldiers never, never allowed themselves to be channeled down existing streets and roads when entering the city. Instead they used satchel charges, tank guns, and tanks as bulldozers to punch holes through lines of houses and through factories. By moving through the insides of existing structures they kept out of the enemy's sight and out of his ambushes, he said.

Armor used in cities can be decisive, but deployment always carries great risk.

COMBAT IN BUILT-UP AREAS 25

The top of a partially destroyed building can provide excellent cover.

But predictions are tough. Houses along main thoroughfares were often targeted, while those behind were frequently spared. Attacking soldiers also avoided remote neighborhoods where no obvious resistance was organized, especially if barriers and minefields were in place. Another lesson for city survivors.

Fortunes of war are indeed fickle. Absolutely no one can really know ahead if they will end up in harm's way. I think of the Englishman so disgusted by World War I he moved to a remote coaling station in the Pacific. Vessels had then begun to burn Bunker-C fuel, not coal, so "nobody will ever bother me here," he reasoned. But, of course, Midway Island became a major battleground in World War II.

As long as they are tall, buildings that are not strategic and less than dominant can successfully be turned into protected fortress-type structures for use by city survivors. Beirut provides several excellent examples. Survivors there often occupied apartments of high-rise buildings whose top two or three floors had been reduced to rubble, either intentionally or by enemy artillery fire. Layers of ruin above provided excellent protection from artillery or mortar fire, while both giving the impression of being a dead building and giving defenders high ground among protective rubble. But there were other considerations.

Was the building damaged to the point of near-collapse? Some residents lived in great danger in this type of rubble. Additionally, past six or eight floors, walking up to an apartment on a daily basis becomes a real chore (obviously no elevators ran). Survivors argue both ways. While hauling in food and water was difficult, these buildings offered high-rise inaccessibility in uncontested neighborhoods and provided great security.

Some movement out of the retreat will be unavoidable. Know ahead that leaving the retreat is accompanied by great danger and that this must be planned for. Sending a boy or girl out for essential food, water, or medicine often presents an unacceptable risk, because torture is a common and, many claim, necessary element of urban warfare. I have spoken with German women who lived in Berlin at the time of the Soviet occupation, who recalled that if they were caught out on the street they were raped often six or eight times before escaping and hiding again.

Rubble produced by enemy artillery and air strikes can hinder the movement of attacking infantry while simultaneously providing cover for defenders. Attacking commanders often attempt to minimize this problem by ordering their troops to torch cities. The success of this device depends entirely on the type of construction and nature of building contents. Under the wrong circumstances there is little to be done to save one's city, urban survivors claim. Some survivors report having been able to remove combustibles while simultaneously putting out fires as they started. Others took shelter in fire-resistant buildings.

With the battle past, some even re-established living quarters in fire-gutted buildings. This doesn't sound terribly practical, but many of these folks reported living through what seemed like horrible, large, citywide fires.

Sandbagged emplacements are recommended to control fire and to afford some protection from small-arms fire. These can be quite clever, including sandbagged overhead racks, frontal barriers, and floors. Often these structures take on the character of gun emplacements. While those who intend to fight with the urban guerrillas need to know the theory behind these, they are mostly unnecessary for city survivors and will not be covered here, except in passing.

Those interested can secure U.S. Army training manuals on urban warfare as reprints from Paladin Press or in their original form from military manual suppliers. Most military manuals are available in local university libraries where they can be freely copied. Look for anything on combat in built-up places.

Not only is warfare likely in cities where we live, it is also like-

COMBAT IN BUILT-UP AREAS

Small, portable weapons that give individuals great firepower will be a decisive factor in urban combat.

ly that this warfare will be bitterly fought. Modern commanders know from past experience that a well-prepared and mutually supported position in a city can usually be defended by a small force. Attackers are likely to suffer heavy losses and perhaps even temporary defeat against a smaller defending force.

At one time wise commanders bypassed built-up areas, allowing defenders be gradually starved out. East of the Mississippi and in Europe, urban development is so extensive that this tactic is no longer considered practical.

In this and most other cases, survival has proven possible if we limit our defense to our own immediate area. Personal defense in cities, especially when the distinction between the military and police is blurred, is complex. More about this in subsequent chapters.

Urban warfare is old hat to some and terrifying to others. Recently some good friends in the militia movement argued at great length that because our military has studied warfare in built-up areas, it was planning to attack Citizen America. In that regard, the topic was terrifying to them. More likely our military studies this situation because it is the one that must be dealt with. We who plan to survive in cities also need to study it to know what lies ahead.

If anything, this situation demonstrates that successful city survival is the ability to remain flexible, creative, resourceful, and knowledgeable under city warfare conditions. It's about knowing how urban warfare will most likely be undertaken and how to pick places least likely to be heavily affected. It's not about banding together to engage in open, violent urban warfare against a common enemy. People surrounded, identified, and cut off will always eventually be destroyed.

Those reporting the greatest success claim that they husbanded and hoarded all their resources so that, after the enemy had passed, they had the necessary supplies to allow them to hunker down for the long haul—the real work of city survival.

Chapter 3

The Government's View of Survivalists

"So, you define a modern, practical survivor as being an individual who is not dependent on government for any kind of help or assistance," a reporter assigned to a nationally known modern men's magazine quoted back somewhat skeptically.

"Yes," says I, "but add in the fact that government help is always intervention, not help. They try to put a human face on things but look how many people have been manipulated, ruined, and even murdered by their own government in the 20th century alone."

Governments never trust freedom-loving, independent citizens.

It seemed especially curious that he had called from New York—not an especially notorious center of freedom or survivalism or individual liberty.

Judging by the trite little collection of shallowness and trivia he eventually came up with for an interview, the fellow really

29

didn't get it. Even as brief as it was, his article was shot through with scorn and ridicule toward survivors or anyone who would ever dream of living free. It was the same day the Albanian refugee crisis hit the front page. People are being murdered *en masse* by their own government and he ridicules anyone who would think of living free from government "help."

I asked which goods and services he personally depended on that came directly from central authorities.

He didn't want to hear it, but Mao, Stalin, Lenin, and even Heinrich Himmler, director and early organizer of the Nazi Schutzstaffel (SS), fully recognized that counter-revolutions traditionally have started in the countryside. Himmler believed it could be a good revolution if it was kept entirely under his personal direction, philosophy, and control. Perhaps this is part of the origin of Mao's and Stalin's intense paranoia regarding rural freedom-loving survival-type individuals. Yet, keep in mind, Lenin predated any serious SS philosophy by at least 10 years. Why he really feared country folks and wanted to herd everyone into cities is probably lost in history. Lenin said it was to industrialize the country. So they became worker bees in his own private hive!

We see it today in our own society. There are people who believe the government can solve problems and are willing to allow others to take control of their lives. There's no question that the bureaucracy still believes that if it herds enough citizens into cities and provides enough essential services, the rank and file can be brought under their control. Substantial amounts of propaganda regarding the indispensability and wisdom of government are a prime ingredient in this formula. Then those who wish to continue this feudal system under their own superior "leadership" can prevail over the rest of us.

This simple little concept in this brief chapter is the core of city survival: Those who are and/or will allow themselves to be wards of the government don't have the slightest prayer of making it in a truly grinchy city-survival situation. In times past it was said, "Understand this concept and live free. Neglect it and become a slave." In cities it's life and death, not just freedom and slavery.

The problem is that city survivors have a greater struggle in

THE GOVERNMENT'S VIEW OF SURVIVALISTS

Observation and police helicopters will be used against city survivors.

avoiding this evil trap. Providing essential goods and services to naturally independent, widely scattered, historically self-sufficient country people is so inefficient that governments that try quickly go broke. Currently few make the effort. There are just not enough people concentrated any place out in the country to be worth dealing with.

Also, I strongly suspect that in our modern times, other than in a few remote and insignificant regions around the globe, there no longer are enough people in the country to carry out a successful counter-revolution.

This does not suggest that government officials are no longer paranoid in the finest Maoist-Stalinist tradition. Although it is not widely known or popularly understood outside certain regions, significant numbers of freedom-loving citizens in Washington state, Oregon, Idaho, and western Montana view current government Wild Lands proposals—which are plans to move people from their rural homes and into cities to allow the land to go back to nature—as being little more than a thinly disguised method of putting the people in the position of becoming wards of the government. The fact that Wild Lands proponents receive huge amounts of under-the-table government money in direct defiance of congressional oversight or approval—very similar to CIA funding during our Vietnam era—does little to calm citizen fears.

Yet changes in our society are occurring at a breathtaking rate. Our military recognizes this truth when it prepares to fight in cities. Unstoppable events, including dramatic advances in technology way beyond our control (and perhaps even our understanding), are push-

The modern Bradley fighting vehicle, often used to deliver a squad of infantry into built-up areas, has more firepower than World War II main battle tanks.

ing all of us into living in built-up areas. These areas are characterized by high population densities and large numbers of buildings, and put us in great danger of dependence on government for goods and services.

But back in New York on the phone with the men's magazine reporter, my question was, "What absolutely vital goods and services necessary to daily existence do you rely on that are provided by the government?"

His answer was a no-brainer in more ways than one. "Absolutely nothing," he quickly thundered back. That these people are all cut from similar cloth should not be a surprise. He was now had by the ears, but he didn't quite know it. Sounded familiar.

"Oh," says I, affecting my best innocence, "then you can own a firearm of some sort, thereby taking personal responsibility for your own immediate security?" Keep in mind it was New York on the line, where personal responsibility for security has been lost for decades.

"Why would I even dream of owning a gun? I don't want to attack anyone," was his instant response. Obviously he was from one of those new touchy-feely type of men's magazines that wouldn't touch articles about guns, cockfighting, cigars, or bear hunting on a bet.

There are those among us who believe that our president's cur-

THE GOVERNMENT'S VIEW OF SURVIVALISTS 33

An actual Soviet tank used by Fidel Castro to crush insurgents.

rent tirade against gun owners is *not* really about diverting attention from his many other shortcomings, but rather a thinly disguised attempt to make average citizens more dependent on government. This theory gains credibility when we realize again that our police forces have no binding legal responsibility to protect us! Citizens have repeatedly tried to sue for damages when they were denied permission to own a gun for self-protection and were subsequently attacked. Suits for damages against their police departments got nowhere.

It's true that Thomas Jefferson believed Americans should own firearms as a final last resort against government officials who oppress them. But in this era of wall-to-wall cities, it may be more than that. There is also the matter of government ownership and distribution—either through direct ownership or indirectly through licensing—of electricity, heat, water, communications (radio, phone, and TV), transportation, and postal services. But self-protection is even more at the core than these.

Numerous experts have pointed out that Stalin could never have murdered and carried out deportations in the Ukraine, Mao in northern China, Pol Pot in Cambodia, or England in Scotland (during their 18th-century war of independence) had average citizens been even modestly well armed.

Aleksandr Solzhenitsyn, author and philosopher, believes the Russian people could have even successfully resisted the secret police and going to the gulags with little more than resolute application of axes, butcher knives, harvesting tools, and meat hooks. Sounds like lots of resoluteness, but his idea is duly noted.

The reporter never did admit to seeing the connection between private firearms and freedom, but he seemed to warm to the idea that official provision of sewer, garbage, and water service could quickly lead to significant control. "Fact is," he said, "I vividly recall our garbage strike and what an incredible mess that turned out to be," he finally admitted.

He did weasel a bit by claiming garbage service was private in New York. "Yes, private, but maintained by a government-enforced monopoly," I suggested. "All they have to do is threaten to pull the company's permit and your garbage collectors will do whatever the bureaucracy wants. You cannot legally go into any business in New York without official sanction," I reminded him.

Water is extremely important to city survivors.

Governments in most places handle waste and garbage. Disposal of these can be a weak link for hiding city survivors.

Downtown Havana, Cuba, where compliant citizens are herded into places of complete subjection.

Failure of supply could be as serious as going without personal protection, and could arguably be as vital or more vital than personal gun ownership. But to claim that garbage is more important than guns is just that.

Other than electric utilities being government-controlled monopolies, is the electrical system in very many big cities in America still directly owned and controlled by the government? During the 1920s and '30s many small, more rural cities developed their own electrical systems—mostly small-scale hydro projects. Currently, even when utility companies are not collectively owned, the authorities can throw their considerable weight around, denying service to anyone they wish. This is exactly how it works in

THE GOVERNMENT'S VIEW OF SURVIVALISTS 35

Cuba, where average citizens don't receive enough power each day to successfully run a refrigerator!

Wise city survivors had best look at their own situations now, before the crisis. What essentials to your life do your central authorities provide? Can they arbitrarily and capriciously cut you off, forcing you into becoming a ward of the state?

Forms of government dependence are not all obvious and may vary in priority according to a person's philosophy. Service may vary from city to city, and from country to country. In Britain and Canada, for example, citizens must go hat in hand to the bureaucracy for permission to have a vasectomy, a hernia repair, or knee surgery. A close friend flew his mother to the United States for a hip replacement because she was too old to receive one in Canada! Bypass surgery is not done in Cuba past the age of 50 because recipients do not have sufficient working life left to give to the state. The United States is headed in that direction. More distressing, some people really believe this is a good thing!

In Beirut, shortly after the very bleak days, private mail courier services sprang up. Again, we must keep our eye on the ball. Establishment of private medical care might be very important. But is mail delivery on our list of absolutes required to sustain life?

On one occasion a woman told my daughter, only half in jest, that she could not envision life without her daily soaps (low-grade melodramatic entertainment). Possession of a functional TV cable, satellite dish, or computer connection might possibly be a requirement for her life. That is certainly not a judgment I wish to make.

Like any other survivors, city survivors must start planning now if they hope to provide their own services. It's very important to note that, on close inspection, we often find many of these services are provided by central authorities. Anne Frank, the young Jewish girl in World War II Holland, almost survived. She wrote that at times a chronic lack of sewage/waste disposal actually threatened their sanity, security, and immediate health.

Personal responsibility and self-reliance require great attention to detail. An unlicensed private nursery in Salem, Oregon, for example, was discovered and summarily shuttered when authorities were tipped off to its existence by the quantity of disposable diapers found in their trash. This is not city survival, but a down-home example of the length to which bureaucrats will go to maintain their control.

Citizens squashed by enemy armor at a watering area.

My list of vital services that may be controlled by the government and for which city survivors should make other arrangements includes the following:

- Sewage systems
- Garbage collection and disposal
- Communications including radio, television, phone, mail, and Internet access
- Fuel
- Medical services
- Utilities such as gas and electric power
- Transportation
- Water
- Food
- Self-defense/security
- Shelter

Of these, only food, water, shelter, and self-defense are definitely on the list of must-haves needed to survive. Others may also be there, depending on one's personal circumstance. My advice is to never, never rely on people who don't give a damn—such as government officials—for something really important.

Chapter 4

Water

"Successful city survivors will have to drink lots of brown and green water."

After hearing this a second and third time from survivors of Berlin and Beirut, it was obvious that this was going to be a very nasty chapter.

It's akin to the social structure in socialistic economies. Everyone is equal, but some comrades are more equal than all the others. Supplies of water are like that! All absolute elements of survival will lead to death when denied, but depending on weather, workload, and physical condition of the survivor, water is the most immediate. Without it you die quickly and cruelly.

The Rule of Threes is an iron rule in the case of city survivors and water.

But there is great cause for hope. In a very few cases, water continues to run from the pipe. It may not be usable without further treatment, but it is something to work with. For purposes of this chapter, though, tap water is not a consideration. Few experienced been there, done that city survivors mention using it.

It isn't an accident of history that many cities in the world were built around natural waterways. Easier transportation using boats and barges in the early days led to that. Cities grew around profitable commerce. Securing adequate potable water may simply be a matter of laying in securely covered, easily filled and cleaned plastic buckets, a carrying yoke, filter racks, purification chemicals, and larger retreat-type storage tanks to be used to haul, treat, and store water from rivers and ponds running through or lying around our cities.

In real life it is seldom that easy. Survival is never particularly easy or convenient. It is not a game for lazy folks who cannot or will not plan ahead.

City survivors must creep unseen into public areas to fill their containers with water from ponds, marshes, and streams.

COLLECTING WATER

Getting to and from a pond, canal, swamp, lake, stream, spring, or any other natural water source may be dangerous. It may not be practical or even possible. Many city survivors recall hauling water over as much as 3 miles one way once a day. Figure that on your return trip, weighed down with water, it'll take you twice as long to cover the same ground. On the return haul, slow-moving, heavily laden water carriers may fall under observation, suspicion, and perhaps enemy fire. Great care and extreme caution are definitely in order.

Cities, especially the shot-up variety, provide great opportunity for cover and concealment. At times, large numbers of people will be milling about, providing even greater confusion. This can be a type of cover and concealment itself. City survivors obligated to haul water from great distances had best pick their route and an emergency alternative, as well as time of day with care, lest they compromise themselves and all the others at the retreat. World War II city survivors in occupied countries were in constant danger of the Gestapo and many instances are on record of food or water gatherers simply disappearing. Like smoke in the wind, no trace was ever seen of them again.

How to keep out of enemy clutches? Here are some suggestions from our been there, done that folks: Plan to leave the retreat at a time of the day when surrounding activity is minimal. Travel by a route that does not cross enemy lines and is least likely to lead to exposure, even if this is a very long, circuitous route. Leave the retreat by a route hidden from view.

Humans can walk at a rate of from 3 to 4 miles an hour. Send two water carriers out together, allowing switching of the heavy return load while still maintaining maximum speed and alertness. When not carrying, the other should act as a slightly forward lookout. Survival is about not being lazy or inattentive to details. Don't pick the shortest route unless it is also safe. Always pick the safest route. At the first sign of danger, abandon hauling equipment to run off and hide.

Undertake haulage in 4- to 5-gallon covered cans balanced on a shoulder pole assembly. Carrying heavy buckets long distances over rough terrain by using only hands and arms is not practical.

Precipitation

Collecting rain and its close cousins, snow and ice, is another good, practical, city-survival water-gathering technique. One observer said that he saw it often in Beirut and even in Karachi, Pakistan. I have personally observed many rainwater collection systems in several Yugoslavian cities.

Modern technology helps loads. But just as water from ponds and rivers must be filtered and purified, so must precipitation be treated. And collecting it is just as risky for city survivors as hauling water.

To catch and funnel falling water we have large sets of plastic tarps strung in almost tent-like fashion. It doesn't take a Phi Beta Kappa to realize that someone is around maintaining and using the device.

Collecting water from rooftops that would normally gush down a drainpipe into a storm sewer is also possible. Use plastic sheets and pipe to direct this water into your holding tanks. No precipitation in a city is particularly sanitary. Catching from rooftops that people may walk on and that may also catch dirt and debris is especially unsanitary. Clean collected precipitation similarly to the way you would treat water from ponds, swamps, rivers, and lakes by using a sand filter rack and bleach.

Those who plan ahead can put together a system to collect rainwater from roofs and gutters.

Except in some particularly sodden parts of the world, rain falls infrequently. Bountiful quantities must be stored when it arrives from the heavens. Plastic barrels weighing about 450 pounds when full are ideal. Do most readers realize how absolutely awful water stored over the long term can become? Thank God few people have to drink out of cisterns these days.

There's a lot of work to be done here. Try to filter and purify precipitation stored in the blue plastic barrels as soon as possible. Let's not even talk about water stored 3 or 4 weeks in hot climates that hasn't already been filtered and chlorinated.

At the first sign of trouble, purchase twice as many large plastic tarps, plastic barrels, and plastic pipes and gutters as you expect to need. All of this is very inexpensive, so there's no need to skimp or cut corners.

Been there, done that people report that out-in-the-open, obvious water collection systems on roofs, in parks, or in parking lots are virtually as much of a threat to survivor security as sending the young men out with buckets. These collection devices are easily spotted by members of the enemy forces, who quickly learn what this is all about. Many really don't like it.

Expect them to respond by posting sentries or by tearing up the collection system, if they can reach it. The end result is often predictable, especially when no backup collection supplies are available. You die from lack of water.

City parks with ponds and streams are found in most cities in the United States.

Ice and snow are sometimes sources of water for city survivors. Just hope you also have an excellent energy supply. Ice and snow as sources of drinking water are not as effective as we might wish. Very few examples of using ice and snow are on record as sources of supply for city survivors. Once

It may be green and stale, but little ponds nestled in parks in our cities can be a source of drinkable water.

melted, snow and ice water should be treated the same as any other scrounged surface water. Great quantities of often scarce energy are required to melt ice. Humans cannot normally pack in enough calories to continually exist on ice water thawed in the mouth. Ice has to be melted first or users sucking on it for hydration will risk hypothermia. Cold-weather native survivors can only use solid ice when they are on an extremely high-calorie diet of mostly animal fat.

PURIFYING WATER

At the retreat, allow any surface water to stand and settle quietly in covered containers for at least 12 hours. This isn't always possible, but it is recommended. Is it necessary to mention that water should be brought from an area of as little pollution and contamination as possible?

When the storm sewer discharge is south and north is just as safe, go north. Yet don't be surprised when this isn't practical. Even though this may be a time of great exposure, fill each container in as sanitary and chunk-free a manner as possible. Our practical objective is a supply of drinking water. It is nice if it has as few big brown lumps and stringy green things as possible, but the objective is life-giving water. Obviously not much water ends up hauled by the fellow who tarries overlong and is shot.

Great numbers of really slick little water purification gizmos are available, mostly from stores selling to recreational survivors, backpackers, skiers, and cyclists. All work nicely, but are expensive and not really designed for long-term city survival requiring purification of hundreds of gallons.

Using a Sand Filter

For practical survival use, we'll need a sand filter rack. After the water has settled for 12 hours, carefully pour the top 90 percent of the water through a sturdy fine-weave cloth and then into the sand filter rack. Discard any really scummy settlings. Thoroughly clean the cloth and bucket, setting them out in the wind and sun for a day or two to purify.

WATER

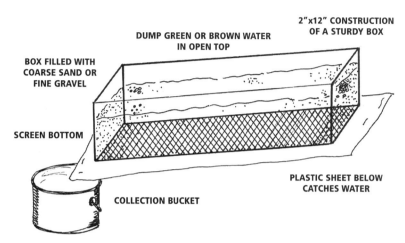

Construct sand filter racks by building a box out of 2-x-10 lumber or something equivalent. Fill with coarse or fine sand. Either will work, but of course they will have much different speeds of filtration. Place the sand-filled rack directly over a seamless plastic sheet. Fastening a piece of screen from an old-fashioned screen door makes the process a bit easier and more convenient. This screen must be replaced every 60 days or so. Let's hope the trouble doesn't last that long.

The sand-filled rack, which could weigh almost 300 pounds, is placed on a slight angle. The plastic collection sheet slopes down into a clean collection bucket. Water poured through the 10-inch-deep sand gradually seeps through to the sheet and runs into the clean storage bucket.

Several additional maintenance chores are in sight here. Unless survivors have an endless supply of clean, new sand with which to replace that in the rack, they will have to empty the filter once a week to spread the sand in a thin layer out in the sun to purify. Sand in heavily used filters will get disgustingly grody very quickly, especially in humid, warm climates or where first settling is rushed or not done at all. Placing very many green and brown chunks in the filter degrades it faster. Carefully clean and dry the underlying plastic sheet.

There is great discussion about specific water purification

methods and chemicals. True enough, most survival stores have material that can kill more little water critters than bleach. If you are so inclined, lay in a large to huge supply of this chemical now. Most people, however, are going to have to use common household bleach because that is what is available and what they can afford and find.

Using Bleach

Common chlorine bleach is in a category with pickling salt for city survivors. At the first sign of trouble, clean out your local store of all you can afford, carry home, and store. It is an essential material. Any excess easily becomes trading stock.

Calcium hypochlorite, available in powder form from most plumbing and hot-tub suppliers, is also a valuable chemical for water treatment. Makers of homemade explosives are already familiar with this stuff. You need add only 1 ounce of calcium hypochlorite per 325 gallons of filtered water to purify it. The cost is about $5 per pound or 31 cents per ounce. But, cost aside, it doesn't keep as well as the laundry bleach. The only way I know to store calcium hypochlorite is to seal it in a heavy plastic bag and then again in a wide-mouth plastic bottle. The best storage life I can get is about 18 months; after that, it swells and is neutralized as a result of sucking humidity out of the air.

Both calcium hypochlorite and sodium hypochlorite can be used to make bleach at home. Generally, survivors are best served who leave their excess hypochlorite supplies safely sealed in plastic bags and jars. But if your hypochlorite starts to go out of condition and/or there is lots of space in the old bleach bottles, consider using the chemical to top up your bleach supply.

Most packets of hypochlorite purchased from plumbing or hot-tub

Common bleach and hot-tub chlorinator found in many stores can be used to help purify water.

suppliers will be about 65-percent strength. Here's how to proceed to make bleach:

There are 128 ounces in a U.S. gallon. Two ounces of hypochlorite chemical in a gallon produces a 1-percent solution. This is not sufficiently strong—it has to be at least 3 percent. Add 6 ounces of chemical to a gallon of clean water, add the stopper, and let it sit overnight. Use this solution at the customary rate of 1 ounce per gallon to purify water. Eight ounces of hypochlorite will produce a 4-percent solution and 10 ounces produce a 5-percent solution.

Poorly filtered, dirty water requires higher quantities of bleach as well as more time to become purified. This explains why we take care to settle and filter our water. Because bleach will be difficult to impossible to replace, we will want to use as little as possible. To purify 1 gallon of water, add 1 ounce of liquid bleach (3- to 5-percent solution) and let it stand for at least 12 hours.

Some survivors I stayed with in northern Kenya rigged a large aquarium-type bubbler to aerate and purify their water. Without bleach it didn't work well. Even with bleach, it is doubtful whether most city survivors could take advantage of this trick. When I lived in Africa, I regularly dreamed of standing in a fresh, flowing mountain stream drinking snowmelt water in cupped hands. After a few weeks of city survival, thoughts of clean, fresh-smelling, cool, untreated water will be in the category of vague dreams of a past life.

One ounce per gallon is a lot less bleach than most publications on the subject recommend. But conservation of scarce supplies is a primary goal here, and taking the time to let water settle is better than using higher quantities of bleach.

If anyone, especially the very young or elderly, acquires a dose of diarrhea, up the bleach a bit. Several M.D. types in our survival culture reckon that most Americans consume unrealistically pure foods and water. As a result, our guts are not immunized against real-world bacterial conditions. Foreign survivors who have built up an immunity have the edge on us in this instance. Don't forget that under the best of circumstances, city survivors are going to drink lots of brown and green water. It's a given.

WELLS

For a brief time in World War I Germany, my father hauled his water from an obscure shallow well. The well was reasonably close as well as being sheltered from view. Because the water was drawn from a depth of only about 20 feet, it probably contained contaminants and growies. At least these weren't large, lumpy green and brown ones, and the family all lived through it. Then somebody stole the handpump. His mother traded for another. Somebody stole that one, too. The pump should have been taken off between uses, but it was too late. Now it was a long hike to the river.

I don't know of a community well left in any large city anywhere in the world. In some places where there are larger, open spaces occupied by gardens, parks, backyards, or even median strips in roadways, it might be possible to drill, drive, or auger in private, shallow wells. When these are put in place, they usually

Some survivors with backyards can install their own shallow wells and old-fashioned hand pumps.

Controls and tanks for a do-it-yourself water system.

provide sufficient water for a family. I recently saw one not too far from the center of London. And a survivor from Atlanta wrote that he had produced a shallow well in his backyard behind a three-story apartment complex! These things do occur, but of course won't unless survivors look for opportunities to put them in place before an emergency.

When much younger I used a gasoline engine power head that slowly turned a 2.5-inch auger shaft to drill shallow wells. It was OK technology for wells no deeper than 25 feet where the underlying material was sandy and rock free. How times have changed! Everything is more sophisticated, expensive, and certain. Deeprock Manufacturing, 2200 Anderson Road, Opelika, AL 36801, sells a small two- or three-man well-drilling outfit, complete with mud pump (to lubricate and flush out the hole) that will go down 200 feet! Other than those living in the arid West, everyone is assured of water using one of these outfits. The cost is about $3,000 for their smallest model, #2000, which will even drill through solid rock. It takes two people about a day to drill their own private well. Frequently these rigs are available from rental shops. In areas where they are commonly used, a good resale market exists.

All well bores must be cased. For ease of operation and speed, use the smallest drill or auger possible that will also produce an adequate sized well hole. Bore a hole about 1 1/2 to 2 inches larger than the well casing. The casing can be plastic if it will slip straight down easily. When additional pounding is required to set the casing, steel is a must. Plastic or steel, a pointed brass well screen is installed on the bottom end of all well casings. Install a well of a size on the very low end of what is common in your area—usually a 1.25-inch one.

Old-fashioned drill augers we used long ago did not have reverse. We quickly learned not to get into this business without a large, rugged set of pipe wrenches with which to back the auger out if stuck by a rock.

Standard power heads are available to rent just about anyplace in the United States. Contractors use them with 12-inch augers to dig postholes. With careful planning, it is possible to purchase 20 feet of 2-inch auger shaft that fits on these standard contractor-type power heads, allowing insertion of a standard 1.25-inch well casing.

How do you tell whether there is water at the bottom of the hole? Pour water into the hollow well pipe. If it rapidly flows away through the sand and gravel screen, there is water below.

Another detail that makes life easier for do-it-yourself well developers: Three or four 7- or 8-foot well-casing sections with appropriate connections are easier to place than trying to insert a single 20-foot length of pipe.

It ain't easy, but shallow wells can also be driven down into sandy, rock-free ground by hand. The presence of tough clay or any coarse gravel or rock precludes using the following method, which is already so much work that I am reluctant to mention it.

The tools required are a 10-pound (or larger) steel maul, two 36-inch steel pipe wrenches, a 5-gallon water bucket, and some very sturdy boxes, logs, or scaffolds to build up a place to work from. Start with three 6-foot lengths of heavy, steel 1.25-inch well pipe. Special heavy-duty drive couplings needed to connect the pipe sections and a special drive cap to protect pipe threads while whacking away at the pipe end are also required. You will also need a special, heavy-duty well point screen made for this type of mauling. These fittings are not common, but all large plumbing shops I know of can order them. If not, try Lehman's Hardware and Appliances, Inc., Box 41, Kidron, OH 44636. Their stuff is a bit pricey but is of very good quality and fully guaranteed. Lehman's sells predominantly to the Amish community and are very nice folks indeed to work with. I recommend paying up promptly, gladly, and without a whimper, no matter what the price.

Deploying three or four stout men, take turns pounding the point and pipe down into the ground. Two things make this marginally easier. Using the two pipe wrenches and a section of pipe over the handle, keep rotating the well pipe and point as it goes down. Keeping the pipe full of water is messy when it is hit, but will marginally lubricate the point as it goes down.

The maximum depth is 20 to 25 feet. Never assume that this will be easy, but in areas where surface water rises to within 20 feet of the ground and where there is no gravel or rock, it works like a champ. No expensive equipment is needed, there's not much mess or fuss, and it can usually be undertaken in an afternoon. It's all we had when I was a kid. Many wells of this type were driven right in our friends' backyards in the middle of town.

Water can, theoretically, be pumped by hand from as deep as 200 feet using special handpumps. These and more practical shallow-well pitcher-and-stand pumps are available from Lehman's Hardware.

What can you do if you have the opportunity to rope-haul fresh drinking water up from a steep canyon or perhaps a very deep abandoned well? Climbing down to the water may be impossible, so what to do?

Lehman's sells a special 2-gallon bucket with a unique valve that opens when it hits the water, closing again automatically when the bucket is withdrawn. A rope the length of the drop is required. It's lots of work using this method, but it may be the only game in town when the water cannot be otherwise reached.

STORING WATER

The need for potable water is of such a high order that an initial emergency storage supply must be provided. Waterbed bladders, cheap fiberglass tanks, blue barrels, or whatever else work nicely, just so long as you don't use those ridiculous small packets and cans that

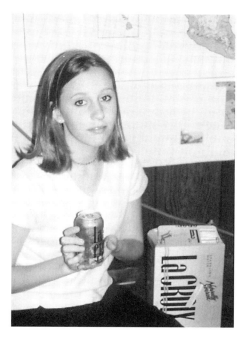

Little cans or bottles of water are not practical for city survivors. The large quantity of trash they create may expose the survivors' retreat.

some survival houses sell. The huge amount of trash generated by these little packets alone may expose the retreat. I personally use a 250-gallon fiberglass tank purchased for $150 (peanuts, given water's importance).

This storage will get you past the onset of an emergency, but it's absolutely not meant as a continuing means of survival. How much water will you need? Figure about 1 gallon a day per person if no one washes anything except teeth and a single cup or plate. As a simple matter of hygienics, this is practical only in the very short run.

In other words, when the sound of gunfire can be heard in the distance, fill all the fiberglass tanks, blue plastic barrels, waterbed bladders, 5-gallon jugs, and whatever else. Uncovered water, as in bathtubs, usually doesn't work. There's too much pollution accompanied by evaporation. I don't even own a bathtub, but if I did, I wouldn't want it full of slimy, green water!

Shallow-well water must be chlorinated, but does not generally have to be filtered. As always, common sense in your individual situation is advised.

SALTWATER

Saltwater will be available to many city survivors. Lehman's has small, reverse-osmosis water purifiers and filters. Model TEC 25D for about $325 looks like it might work. Under normal conditions it is rated at 18 gallons per day. I called Lehman's to find out whether this unit would function as an emergency small-scale desalination plant. One person said "probably," another "might," and the third, most knowledgeable, guy said, "Probably not, because ocean water carries salt concentrations that are too high." I personally would like to field-test this outfit. Let's say it cleaned half its rated capacity, or 9 gallons per day, and that the membrane lasted 1 year rather than 3 (replacements cost about $100). These would be good units for some city survivors. The only restriction is that a water pressure of 40 pounds per square inch is required to operate. This pressure could be achieved by generator-run electric pumps or by a 2-story column of water in a standpipe. I live 500

WATER

Inexpensive and small desalinization plants such as this one in Cabo San Lucas, Mexico, provide potable water. Reduction in unit size is occuring, but most are still too large and expensive to be of practical use for individual survivors.

miles from the nearest saltwater, so field-testing a model TEC 250 probably won't happen.

Common reverse-osmosis desalinization units require very little power. Smaller and smaller sizes are increasingly on the market. I looked at one in Cabo San Lucas, Mexico, that cost U.S. $175,000 installed! It produced 80 gallons of pure, fresh water per minute. Practical for some cheap, deserted islands, but certainly not for most city survivors.

One fellow survived several weeks under really desperate conditions in Mombasa, Kenya. He had made a tiny distillery unit that produced about a gallon per day, but his method doesn't sound particularly practical because of the vast amount of energy required. He soldered a long coil of 3/8-inch flexible copper pipe to the lid vent of a 16-quart pressure cooker pot. During the cool of the evening he slowly boiled away salt water, allowing water vapors to condense in the tube. Mere cupfuls of water were all he got. Had he not been able to supplement this with rainwater, he probably would have been toast.

BUYING WATER

In aggressively capitalistic Beirut, water sellers quickly took to the streets after the city collapsed. Theirs was a profit motive that ended up saving lives. They trucked in relatively safe, pure drinking water they loaded at outlying springs and wells and sold it by the liter. While you can't depend on entrepreneurs appearing, unless you are in a previously hard-core socialistic area with few remaining entrepreneurs, it is reasonable that such suppliers will quickly evolve.

But you can't always count on the marketplace. I know about the tremendous importance of this firsthand. It involved my being sent to Algiers on business. Really the end of the earth. There were many, many things to do, all heavily hindered by the fact that I had to spend large blocks of time each morning in search of drinking water. The climate was hot and loathsome, requiring lots of water. Much against my will, the experience became deeply educational.

After 3 days I had a regular route moving from shop to shop, inquiring about the day's supply. No Wal-Marts in Algiers or anywhere in Algeria. For unfathomable reasons, the owner of one obscure little shop or stall might have a liter bottle to sell, when previously he just shook his head. Price was about $1.80 but I certainly didn't quibble.

Usually only a single bottle was available; when it was a half-liter, I continued the march. For about 10 days I lived on 2 liters of purchased bottled water per day. Most days it took 3 hours to line up a supply.

I'm sorry to report that finally, good old intrepid Ragnar was done in by the Algerian system. No busi-

In many places throughout the world, private suppliers with transport trucks step in to provide safe drinking water when other supplies fail.

Downtown Algiers, where the author wandered from shop to shop each day searching for bottled water.

ness could be done; everything was too inefficient. I booked the next flight out. Back in Paris I sat in a tub for 3 hours!

City survivors often talk about stealing needed supplies. Of lining up with the enemy to receive water from the supply truck, of breaking into factories, or hospitals, and so forth, to appropriate supplies. These targets of opportunity may work on a temporary basis, but along with windmills, eating seaweed, apples, or whatever else are not considered here. The Rule of Threes requires that we plan for what at the time appears to be a certain source.

Chapter 5

Sources of Energy

Mannan Sheikh was 12 years old when Britain dissolved its Indian Empire on Friday, August 15, 1947. Independence granted to the subcontinent led to immediate, serious—often vicious and irrational—violence. Mannan, a Muslim, vividly remembers the terror, bloodshed, pain, and great destruction as Hindus and Muslims sorted themselves out into two separate countries. Mannan and his family walked from their previous homes in New Delhi, India, to their new place in Karachi, Pakistan.

I asked what they did for fuel along their exit route.

Downtown Karachi, Pakistan, filled with refugees after Britain's dissolution of the Indian Empire.

"We scrounged and stole it," he responded softly. "Those of us who did it best lived the best. We had sticks, grass, camel dung, and some kerosene with which to warm ourselves and our food each morning with all the tens of thousands similarly engaged. It is little wonder governments take such a dim view of refugees, treating them so horribly."

Sources of fuel required to sustain life will certainly be on almost everyone's list of threes. I cannot imagine a situation where this vital requirement is taken lightly and there will still be survival.

Some city survivors will be located in sufficiently warm places that they will require little more than a sweater at night and some fuel to cook with and to warm wash water. In many U.S. cities, even at their nastiest time of the winter, survivors will need do little more than put on an extra sweater. In other places in the northern United States and Europe, great quantities of fuel and the means to use it will be essential for city survival.

Rural survivors generally rely on stored sources of energy. Several thousand gallons of fuel oil, large cylinders of LP gas, barrels of gasoline, and piles of coal are common. In many instances these comprise only a year's to 18 months' supply. Anything more than that must be scrounged up from renewable sources such as a seam of coal in the hill behind the house, firewood, windmills, or even solar energy of one sort or another.

Renewable sources are not as far-fetched nor as impossible for city survivors as one might initially suppose. Storage and renewal of energy in a city is possible for those who plan ahead. Many are doing it right now.

A city survivor in Knoxville, Tennessee, wrote to tell me about the seam of low-grade coal he discovered in a roadcut about a mile from his home. His intention was to stockpile about 30 to 40 burlap bags of purchase coal and then to strip coal from the seam as needed. He said that probably no one else knew about this little "gold mine of energy."

Here is another unique source of fuel for city survivors that readers have written about. A survivor from Minneapolis suggests stockpiling packed compressed and wrapped bales of common peat as sold by garden supply stores. He uses a small cast-iron stove both to cook and to heat his small retreat area in the big city. One 40-pound, 4-cubic-foot bale heated his basement apartment for about 3 weeks, he claims. On that basis, eight bales would just about see him through the cold time. More remarkable, he also found a way to renew his peat supply.

SOURCES OF ENERGY 57

Some properly situated survivors can collect native coal from large or small seams of coal for use as emergency fuel.

Where corn is abundant, it can be used as a fuel source.

An old, now-drained swamp lies to the north of his built-up area. It contains a vein of peat 40 feet deep in many places. During the summer dry time he carefully dug several large trailer loads of wild peat, which he took back to his apartment. Attempts to sun-dry the material on plastic tarps were only modestly successful, he claims. Still, the material burns, cooks, and heats just fine, but it is very difficult to compact and store, he reports. Also, it is messy. I reminded him that while not perfect, it was an energy source he could live with.

Perhaps the important concept for city survivors involves looking around with a knowing, intelligent eye. Other renewable sources of energy besides miscellaneous sticks, grass, firewood (from parks and arboreta), animal dung, old furniture, garbage, and refuse are out there. Several friends report successfully using dried kernel corn and wheat in pellet-type stoves. Seems like an incredible waste of something that should be eaten. But we never know. How far do you live from grain terminals? The claim is made that no city dweller in Portland, Oregon, lives more than a mile from a grain terminal. Turning dried grains into a flammable energy source takes some additional stove maintenance and operator skill, but it apparently is a feasible plan.

But, back to advanced purchase and fuel storage in a city. History shows that city survivors in the very center of an intensely built-up area may not be able to take advantage of very many renewable sources of energy, and they may not be able to store same with ease. But, they can definitely store some energy for emergency use and there is always the possibility of some scrounging.

Right now, city survivors are unobtrusively laying in bales of peat, tanks and drums of diesel oil, cans of gasoline, and stacks of firewood in the backyard, garage, or against the side of the duplex. Purchase of older, used, steel 250-gallon fuel oil tanks is possible. These are common in places where natural gas lines have recently been laid and homeowners have converted their oil burners. Used fuel oil tanks are still common in junkyards and at heating and plumbing shops. Right now, there are at least six in a building recycler's yard within 2 miles of my desk. I have purchased many of these

An emergency 1,000-gallon fuel oil tank waits at the retreat.

Firewood is a renewable resource for those who know how to gather and use it.

used tanks in good, sound condition for $50 each. I set them in the garage, the basement, or along the side of the duplex where I had them filled with oil. After several weeks the outside tanks blended in with their surroundings. No one paid them notice any longer.

The important concept for city survivors is to not to make assumptions. Storage of energy is probably possible and it probably won't be very high-tech or complicated.

How much to store? The ugliness in India took 2 years to pass. Madrid, during the Spanish Civil War, was besieged for about 8 months, and Berlin was back to some idea of normal after an especially harsh winter season (of about 6 months). Using Berlin as an example in this case is tough. City survivors would have had to act at least 3 years ahead of total collapse.

Most been there, done that folks recommend a 1 year's supply of energy under storage. Of course, this amount should be supplemented by at least two other independent and separate sources of supply. The Rule of Threes is never suspended.

Knowing how these energy sources will be used at your specific retreat is very important. Many concepts are workable, but not particularly practical or efficient. I looked at an inner city apartment retreat recently. There was a workable fireplace in which fuel could be burned for cooking. Not wise, it seemed. Certainly meals would be prepared, but little to no heating of the room would be accomplished.

USING STOVES AND HEATERS

I advise the purchase of a simple, small, inexpensive cast-iron stove and about 6 feet of vent pipe plus an elbow to run the pipe up the chimney. Total cost, including a fireproof mat to set the stove on, about $450. Without the fireplace, the little stove could have been set in the middle of the room with vent pipe out through a hole cut in a side wall. Larger vent pipes additionally heat the room and cool sufficiently by the time they exit the wall, so they pose little fire danger. Little heating and cooking stoves of this type are a bit tricky to operate, but survivors learn surprisingly fast. The stoves' additional charm is that they will burn just about anything, even diesel fuel, if set up correctly.

To efficiently burn diesel fuel in a cast-iron stove made for logs, coal, and other such combustibles, construct or scrounge a heavy pot or iron/steel container as large as possible that will sit inside the stove. Fill it two-thirds full of diesel oil. Place a piece of burning cardboard or heavy paper in the oil. Fumes from the warmed oil will burn at the top with a low-grade, warm glow. Intensity and heat output plus oil consumption are controlled by the air intake in the stove and outlet on the rear stove vent. These are very much similar in operation to commercial "spark heaters."

Common fireplace inserts or stoves can be converted into "spark heaters" by using a large pan full of fuel oil. Fumes from the oil are burned to produce low-grade, economical heat.

Because they require storage of bulky, tough-to-handle, highly refined kerosene, I am not particularly fond of the little oriental space-heating stoves often sold by Wal-Mart and Home Depot under the trade name of Sun (or something similar). Numerous city survivors, including my son, claim they will use these because of the following:

- They are inexpensive to purchase and install.
- They are commonly available without hassle from local hardware and builder supply outlets.
- They require no outside source of electrical energy.
- They nicely heat a modestly well-insulated four-room apartment.
- They are light and easily portable.

Similarly informed people often differ in their opinions. And keep in mind that city survivors, including me, may pay with our lives for bad decisions and lack of prior planning. I dislike these heaters because of these factors:

- The fuel is expensive and difficult to find and store.

SOURCES OF ENERGY

- They have a relatively low energy output that can only be used to heat. No cooking can be done on these units.
- The kerosene fuel has a relatively low energy output per gallon and can only be used in these little stoves.
- These heaters are cantankerous, difficult, and short-lived in an environment screaming for rugged simplicity and long life.

I like common diesel fuel that can be used in both machinery and heaters. Diesel is the likely fuel you will get from military fuel dumps, old petroleum distribution points, abandoned vehicles, and street merchants. Diesel is what you will probably store in 55-gallon barrels or in the big tank next to the fence.

Some very nice, entirely commercial space heaters are available for city survivors who want to heat with diesel fuel. First, be sure it isn't possible to scrounge one of the old army surplus, collapsible, multifuel stoves. A few new ones with only storage corrosion are still out there. Second, consider converting a small cast-iron stove to use oil as previously mentioned. These units are very versatile.

Local plumbing/heating/hardware people will have diesel-oil-burning stoves and space heaters. Stoves run on oil fumes. They require no electricity and are very reliable (Oil is gravity-fed from a storage barrel to the stove). Most weigh about 200 pounds and will heat a small house (six rooms) nicely. They cost about $1,200.

Try Wolf Steel, 9 Napoleon Road, RR 1, Barrie, Ontario, Canada L4M 4Y8 if your local dealer doesn't have something suitable. Wolf Steel manufactures a stove called the Napoleon. It's expensive, but very nice and extremely simple.

Oil space heaters use electric pressure pumps and high-capacity fans to turn diesel oil into heat. They range in price from $160 to $2,000 (for great, giant units used to heat airplane hangars). These are nice units if power is available. Order from Granger Supply if you draw a blank at your local dealer. Granger has one outlet or more in every state in the union.

Oil space heaters are often used in hunting camps, summer homes, garages, and barns. City survivors may wish to purchase their heaters now to learn how to operate them. I, for instance, have burned up three of these units when they accidentally became unplugged. Chickens sitting on the power cord burned one and also the chicken house. Who said true intelligence only comes from actually doing something? This sure is true of my experience with oil space heaters.

Stoves require venting, but no electricity. Space heaters are not vented, but consume lots of electrical energy.

GENERATORS

This brings up another important point. Do city survivors need to plan to have some small amounts of self-generated electrical power? Based on advice from the been there, done that crew, the answer is yes. But it needn't be a large amount. A small generator—perhaps 4,000-watt capacity—is almost a necessity to run a heater, the freezer, the fridge, or perhaps a water pump on a short-term basis, they claim.

Because city survival involves so much long, grueling, hard work that continues into the night, it may be tempting to run a light. This is not recommended unless you are willing to risk a mortar round down the elevator shaft, or unless all soldiers have left the city and no danger from aggressors remains.

The noise from generator operation can also attract attention. It wasn't quiet, but almost, during city survival in metro Manila, where the power frequently and repeatedly died. I vividly recall the noise of various generators, small and great, as they fired up.

Tracking down one noisy generator among many might be impossible. Finding a lone unit in operation in the middle of a quiet city would be relatively easy unless it was high up and deep within a building. Some city survivors mention using snipers or armed guards to protect their rain-collection systems and generators, but I would suppose it is the better part of wisdom not to plan to get into firefight situations.

The problem with simple little 4,000-watt generators is that for true city survivors, they really don't cut it. After long, long years of living with generators, I have concluded only diesel-fired models made for commercial application are practical for survivors.

Gasoline, for gasoline engines, is difficult to store. Its volatility is

SOURCES OF ENERGY 63

Many survivors who have reviewed their options have concluded they must use a generator.

LP gas heaters are useful in some survival circumstances. This city survivor has just refilled her small, portable LP gas tanks from the larger tank.

a storage curse in the medium to long run. Diesel fuel packs a great deal more energy per gallon, and diesel generators are virtually always continuous-duty, industrial types. They initially cost more, but will run dramatically longer before wearing out and breaking down.

Most generators doing city survival duty are plugged directly into the appliance they are powering. By contrast, large, 8- to 10-kilowatt generators at country retreats are often backfed into the entire power complex at the retreat. Backfeeding is very illegal some places, and won't work at all in small apartments that are part of a large building complex.

When backfeeding, the main power panel fuses are removed from the retreat power box. This keeps the generator power from feeding back out across the transformer into the line again, where it can be a life-threatening hazard. A sort of heavy extension cord with two male plugs is used to backfeed power from the generator's 220-volt circuit to a commercial welder, shop, or electric range outlet.

Storing Fuel

Diesel oil isn't always used to generate power. Recently two city survivors I was working with buried 1,000-gallon LP gas tanks in their garage, right in the city. This is very illegal in some places. These city survivors have another source of energy should they need it. This is another good example of city storage of energy for those who act resolutely.

Small LP gas space heaters are available virtually everywhere. LP gas heaters are inexpensive, mobile, easily maintained, and effective if some way exists to refill the little 1- and 5-gallon pressure tanks they run on. They require no electricity, and they are not obvious.

Is the installation of a 1,000-gallon LP pressure tank advisable for city survivors? One of the friends who put his tank in intends to run his generator on LP gas. Many gasoline generators will also run on LP gas. The power output using LP gas is lower, especially at higher elevations, but the versatility is nice. Many tank owners also have a tank filler hose and fitting installed so that they can refill smaller tanks.

LP gas suppliers are reluctant to sell large pressure tanks outright. They will lease, which could end up working against survivors who may suddenly have their tanks "recalled." Guaranteed, you won't bury anybody's leased LP gas tank. It will almost certainly take at least 8 months of persistent pushing to finally take delivery of your own private LP gas tank. That's how it worked with me, and with my two acquaintances who buried their tanks in the city.

One thousand gallons of LP gas will generally last about 1 year when used to run a generator in intermittent service. Cost is about $1,600 for the tank and about $850 to fill the first time. Whether or not this is practical depends on each individual. Is there enough personal energy to push this kind of project through to completion, the money to do it correctly, a place to hide the tank, and application within the retreat?

SOLAR POWER AND WINDMILLS

Solar power, windmills, and perhaps small hydroelectric pro-

SOURCES OF ENERGY

A bank of expensive, high-maintenance storage batteries are a necessary part of a solar power system.

jects are trendy now among city survivors. They are frequently mentioned as the 21st century's answer to individual electrical power in cities. Solar power systems are being installed around the world with increasing frequency. As a result, we know a bit more about them. I looked at three recently. All are in smaller cities: Pullman, Washington; Kodiak, Alaska; and Boulder, Colorado.

The system in Boulder is extremely simple, with a hot-water pipe on the roof warmed by the sun. Given installation, price, simplicity, and lack of maintenance, it may still be the most practical. Small, discreet copper pipes laid on a south-sloping roof section warm the water, which heats the house. Its installation 20 years ago was very inexpensive. Most people who visit the house are not aware the system exists. Over its life, the system has saved at least $200 to $300 per year in energy costs, the owner claims.

The extent to which a real solar power (sunlight-to-electricity) system would stick out, compromising a retreat, is still subject to debate. One owner says people never notice. The other says it's obvious what he's doing. One thing is certain—if an enemy observed and decided to destroy a retreat's solar power system, damage in a survival sense would be serious. All hope of having electrical power would be gone if this were the only means of providing it.

Solar panels have come down in price, but they constitute only a small fraction of the expense of an entire system.

Control and converter panels are the heart of a solar power system.

In other words, even though it works like a champ, solar power still may not be practical for city survivors.

Great misconceptions continue to be attached to solar power. The greatest of these claims is that it will become more practical and cost-efficient as prices for solar panels continue to fall. Well, yes—but really, no—might be the real best answer to this one. Most of the very high cost of a solar power system is *not* in the panels!

The system in Pullman, Washington, that I examined very closely cost about $65,000 complete. On a bright summer day it supplies enough power to run a large house, a guesthouse, and an extensive shop.

Of this 65 grand, 16 solar panels at $375 each total $6,000. The inverter needed to turn the 48-volt direct current to 220-volt alternating current costs right at $9,800. Forty-eight-volt direct current is produced because of its easy storage in twenty-four 2-volt lead acid batteries.

It's another fallacy that solar panels generate enough electricity on cloudy, short, or wintry days for any practical direct use. This fellow spent more than $9,000 on storage batteries alone. There were also automatic combiner boxes, transfer switches, power panels, and several hundred feet of very expensive, very heavy-gauge wiring. Add another minimum $25,000 to the system for this stuff alone.

His system automatically took power from the solar system till the latter could no longer keep up, then from the grid, and then from batteries. When all of these failed, a diesel generator kicked in. (The diesel generator was not included in the price of the system.) I liked his system, but he only had 300 gallons of diesel oil in reserve.

It seems likely that this is a workable solar power system for real big-city survivors only if they can accommodate the expense. One thing is certain—it would be an injustice and fraud for me to try to set out a specific system that would perform in any reader's personal circumstances. The one thing I know about solar power today is that is still very, very complex and, overall, very expensive.

However, many people are installing solar power systems specifically designed for their application. In Kodiak, Alaska, we were 12 miles from the grid. Bringing in power costs at least $10,000 per mile. There'd be no chance for any electricity here if it were not for solar power.

Windmills, similarly, are more complicated than many people believe. They also require collection boxes, storage systems, and wiring. The man in Pullman intends to put in a windmill if the city fathers will allow it. (This is university country.)

In conclusion, solar power and windmills are currently practical for city survivors. But great diligence during the research phase, as well as deep pockets, will continue to be required. My suggestion is to become familiar, at least in part, with solar power so that you can install the system you need when you can.

Start the process by subscribing to Home Power Magazine, Box 520, Ashland, OR 97520. Home Power's real strengths are its main advertisers. Without a magazine of this type, we have no idea where to go for needed component supplies. I have written to the magazine suggesting a decrease in articles and an increase in advertising, which is of much greater value.

SCROUNGING

Instead of owning a generator, many city survivors steal electricity. I was skeptical, but several been there, done thats said yes, they had tapped into a factory or government office line for their own retreat use. Seems like an overly dangerous process, but survival is not a safe business, especially in the city. Stealing electricity has the charm of not having to fool with a generator.

For those who fail to preplan, what about stealing or scrounging other energy supplies? Experienced city survivors believe there is more opportunity to scrounge energy in the city than out in the country. One can only hope this device does not encourage or become an excuse to neglect preplanning of storage and caching.

Storing 55-gallon drums of emergency gasoline or diesel is not difficult using a common steel barrel.

Looking in abandoned vehicles, at military fuel dumps, at old tank farms, and at construction sites have all been mentioned. But what about gathering combustibles such as boards, pieces of plastic, and charcoal scavenged from abandoned buildings? Perhaps a wooden warehouse lies near your retreat, or trees from the park, or tires from vehicles. I burned tires in my shop stove for years. It was a pain to keep cleaning the stove, and everybody for miles could see the dense smoke, but this was the only downside. The upside was that the tires and their heat were absolutely free. Do the best you can to

A small electric-drill pump is essential to pull fuel from large storage tanks.

SOURCES OF ENERGY 69

They may only have a gallon or two each, but energy-hungry city survivors may siphon some gasoline for their use from these types of machines.

vent the fumes from burning tires or plastic, which can be toxic.

Ever wonder why the Germans in the old East Berlin revered their old linden trees? They were the only older trees that survived. For some reason every other tree in the entire city—both east and west—had ended up as fuel in somebody's stove.

If there are parks and tree-bearing green strips that may yield burnable fuel near at hand in your city, laying in an ax, handsaw, or even small chain saw may be extremely wise. These tools are also useful when scrounging wood out of damaged buildings. As trading stock they would be hard to beat.

Khartoum, Sudan, is a city that has been in perpetual collapse for at least 15 years. No fuel is available from government or private vendors. But this has not slowed entrepreneurs working in the black market. One sees them on street corners and pedaling around on their bicycles selling gasoline, diesel, and kerosene in old liter-size Coke bottles. A few sell fuel measured out of 5-gallon containers into your container. Wholesalers, no doubt. There were also dozens of women with small bundles of split wood branches, bags of charcoal, and animal dung. This brings two more concepts of importance to city survivors into view.

Planning Ahead

The first is perhaps obvious to the point of being trite, but should not be overlooked. City survivors might be able to purchase fuel containers after the start of a crisis, but I wouldn't recommend planning to try it. Purchase now when they are cheap and available. Store three or four 5-gallon containers to transport diesel and as many for gasoline as seems appropriate. You may delay filling these till you hear the guns, but these containers are mostly for transport and scrounging or for transport from stored supplies. Major quantities of gasoline and diesel should be stored in 55-gallon barrels or in 250-gallon steel tanks, not in little 1- and 5-gallon containers.

Learning to Trade

The second is that more than any other class of survivor, city survivors have the opportunity to purchase or trade for needed supplies of everything. Unlike survivors out in the open country where few people live and there are even fewer accumulated survival goods and tools, there will be an abundance in cities. An incentive such as cash or trade goods will bring these items out.

This leads to another basic rule of survival—whether you're in the city or country doesn't make a difference. Survival for everyone is possible. Random events produce some real surprises. Yet, down through history, those who have their financial houses in order will generally survive best.

What is also being implied is that cash and trade goods might be one of the better sources of energy for city survival. Trading goods is a complex subject. See Chapter 10 for more ideas.

Some of these scrounged sources for fuel will require the use of small, portable pumps, probably like the $4.95 plastic one currently on my electric drill. It regularly pumps diesel oil up to 6 feet out of an underground tank. A minuscule amount of electricity is required. Currently I get this from a wall socket, but a 12- to 110-volt vehicle inverter designed to plug into my car's cigarette lighter socket would also work.

There is also the possibility of finding coal in an old electricity generating plant storage area or along railroad tracks where

SOURCES OF ENERGY

City survivors will require large supplies of matches.

steamer coal was once hauled. This was one of several sources of energy for my dad's family during their stay in World War I-era Germany. Fortunately, they lived close to a rail switching yard. But this could have been deadly had the Allies ever started bombing the way they did in World War II.

Been there, done that folk mention mountains of coal at factories in larger cities quickly overtaken by collapse. These mountains of coal quickly walked off, they claimed. So be one of the first to discover this largesse.

Bunker-C, a very thick grade of almost crude oil, is used by many power generation plants. Bunker-C has one of the highest energy-to-volume ratios of any fuel. It is so viscous that it must be heated to 40 degrees before it will run through a pipe. City survivors who scrounge this stuff should mix it with sawdust, leaves, or wood chips to produce a humble, homemade sort of fuel bar. Burn these in the open as a sort of supercharged campfire log.

Burning asphalt from the street was the most exotic energy source I could discover. People in some eastern Russian cities have torn up the blacktop layered on their streets and burned it to cook food and keep warm. Certainly a low-intensity, smoky, sooty deal, but if it's the only game in town, it's the only game in town.

In conclusion of this very important chapter, please recall again that it is dramatically easier to start a cooking/heating fire with matches. Keep a huge supply on hand in your emergency supplies.

Also, keep several dozen small throwaway butane lighters as well as a few scratch-type flint sparkers.

Matches aren't glamorous or high-tech, but they're so handy when every second counts in the fight to stay alive.

Chapter 6

Food

Average Americans, even those who are somewhat self-sufficient, firmly believe that survival in the city is impossible.

I encountered such a couple recently from Spokane, Washington, who flat-out told me, "If there are serious disruptions, we are all going to die." Spokane is only a modestly sized city, but she couldn't make up her mind whether to nod her head ("yes, we are all going to die") or shake it from side to side ("we don't have a prayer").

Maybe yes and maybe no, I always respond. My father survived World War I in a very big city in Germany. Abdullah, an exchange student, made it right through the worst of Beirut, and Martin Fischer's grandmother lived through the entire Soviet occupation when she was a younger woman and wouldn't dare leave the house.

"But what did these people eat?" is always the response.

"Same thing survivors out in the country eat," I tell them.

Survivors—city or country—have a Rule of Threes with which they must operate. This means that, for every one of life's absolute needs, they must make advance provision by three separate and distinct methods. City or country, renewable food is provided through storing supplies, gardening, raising livestock, hunting and gathering, scrounging, purchasing, or bartering.

Pick any three. They all have worked in the past and will work again for those willing to make them work.

Hunting and gathering inside a city is possible. I asked a couple from rural Kenya whether tribal taboos prohibited their eating dogs, cats, and rats in a survival situation. "No," she responded, "we can eat those animals even outside of survival. It's critters with scales, like fish, snakes, and even chicken that are taboo."

Their prohibitions were not nearly so severe as those found among Muslims, but they could—nevertheless—lead to some nastiness. She quickly assured me that she often ate fish. "Grandma still won't eat them," she said, "but I have no problem. Thankfully these taboos are in retreat."

FOOD FROM LAKES AND PONDS

City or country, it has always been my recommendation based on long experience and observation in dozens of countries around the world that the first, best place for survivors to look for a meal is in bodies of water lying near at hand. Swamps, ponds, rivers, lakes, and even lagoons lying within cities all have potential. There are fish of several kinds, ducks, geese, herons, frogs, crayfish, turtles, and perhaps even muskrats and beaver.

Fish

We have a much more profound concept here than most city survivors realize. I returned to Cuba, where I had spent some of my youth, in the spring of 1994 and again in 1996. Some of the Cubans I met were hungry even for a small chunk of meat or fish. Many were thin to the point of malnourishment from lack of protein. At the same time I noticed that the rivers and lakes were overrun with lunker largemouth bass. Seems nobody had fished for them for 30 years or more. These bass could easily have been trapped or even taken using sport-hunting techniques to some extent. Maybe the locals' apathy was due to their ingrained dependence on the government. Other than begging, no Cuban I met seemed willing to seize an opportunity to feed himself or herself by taking personal responsibility.

In many instances sport-hunting and fishing techniques violate

FOOD

the basic Rule of Survival Thermodynamics. Remember, this iron rule says a survivor cannot ever put more energy into a survival project than is taken out in the form of food, fuel, and fiber. It's the same for sport fishing unless the fish are so abundant that one is caught on virtually every cast.

Even if there is uncertainty about whether fish live in a pond, river, or lake, it will cost little to check the water out by construction and deployment of a fish trap. Sometimes, but certainly not always, it is possible to sit quietly in a hidden position near a body of water to observe evidence of fish firsthand. They may be seen rising to the surface for bugs, roiling around in shallow places, creating underwater ripples, or even swimming about.

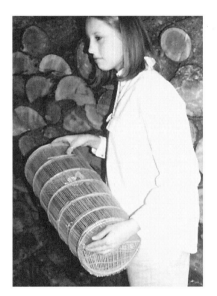

Fish traps are giant cylinders made of chicken wire or, in a few cases, wooden slats or hardware cloth. One end of the cylinder is covered with a chicken-wire door. A long, thin,

These small Asian fish traps are handmade of split bamboo. They are basically large cylinders (top left) with funnel entrances (bottom left) on one end and a door for retrieving the catch (right) on the other. Traps made of chicken wire are made on the same pattern.

tapered cone of chicken wire is inserted in the other end. Fish attracted by bait inside the trap swim into the cone. Once they clear the funnel at its narrow end inside the trap, they are had. Fish are insufficiently smart to figure their way back out again.

Use mesh with 1- to 2-inch openings to build fish traps. Larger mesh sorts smaller fish out, allowing them to escape and fatten up. When survivors are very hungry or do not control the pond, they may elect to construct their fish traps of 1/2-inch chicken wire so that every edible morsel is retained. Very small, fine-meshed traps of this basic design are used to catch 2-inch minnows and 4-inch crayfish.

In times past, we were able to purchase 6-foot-wide chicken wire. This item seems to have gone the way of dinosaurs. With practical limits of weight and portability, bigger fish traps are better. The initial cylinder forming the body of the trap should be at least 3 feet in diameter and 6 feet long.

About 9 running feet of chicken wire or mesh is needed to form a cylindrical tube 3 feet in diameter. If it is only 4-foot-wide wire, purchase and construct a second tube of 2, 3—even 4—feet that is securely sewn with thin wire end to end. Any length cylinder can be made by combining two or three.

At its widest, the entrance cone should attach smoothly to the 3-foot-diameter cylinder body. Quickly taper the cone down to about 3 or 4 inches inside the cylinder, depending on size of fish targeted. The small end of the cone should be capable of being bent and adjusted as needed. This wire cone should extend into the trap about two-thirds the trap's length. Use heavy-gauge #9 wire to strengthen and support the trap as required. This wire can be deployed as hoops around the outside of the cylinder, or the ends, or as supports in the core.

Again, using chicken wire, construct an end for the tube. This flat piece should fit reasonably tightly, keeping the catch inside while still allowing easy access to clean out interred fish. I have caught as much as 30 pounds of fish in a single trap over a 3-day period in traps like these.

Never assume that any pond is cleaned out of fish. During colder periods, fish eat little and move very sluggishly. They may reject any bait till next week when the weather and the water warm slightly. Ideally, bait should be a small can of cat or dog food punctured hundreds of times. Old fish heads, cat guts, fish entrails, and whatever else come to hand to which fish might be attracted can be used. Often I use old roadkills.

Little fish and crayfish swipe soft or fragile small baits out of the trap. This argues in favor of a smaller mesh trap or large, solid baits. Set the trap in a deep hole in a river, or out 12 to 15 feet into a lake.

Exercise caution setting these traps out, even when enemy observation is unlikely. Supposed friends may appropriate the trap's largesse for themselves. Often I throw these fish traps out without retrieving lines attached. This is a more secure system. Retrieval for checking, emptying, and rebaiting is done with a single grappling hook on a line. Without this gear, it is impossible to check these traps even if you know exactly where they are. Attaching a neutral-colored piece of poly line is not as safe regarding detection by the enemy but will make it easier to haul in your catch. Attach this line out of sight to a root or branch a foot or more under water. But don't check your traps too often; continually hooking and hauling in the trap is destructive.

Turtles

These basic-style fish traps modified slightly to a 4- or 6-inch cone opening can also be used to catch turtles. Where they are found, turtles are good food for city survivors. They are often found in great numbers in swamps where there are few or no fish. Catching turtles in traps is a bit tricky. Improperly set traps will drown and waste turtles. One end of the trap has to be up on the bank an inch or two out of the water to provide them a place to breathe. Exposed ends of turtle traps can be hidden a bit with reeds and grass, but hiding is not as easy as fish traps that are 6 feet under the water.

Solid, old, smelly roadkills make excellent bait for turtle traps.

Turtles are dressed for cooking by cutting the bottom shell away from the critter through the soft underbelly hinge. This exposes neck, leg, backbone, and tail meat. Turtle muscle continues to twitch even in the frypan an hour after butchering.

Scooter or box turtles have solid shells which, in most cases, must be sawed away. Not much meat on these guys, but enough for a pot of excellent soup.

Catching turtles by hook and line is probably preferable to using traps if the hooks can be rigged unseen and then retrieved after making a catch. Turtles can be caught on unattended setlines, but these lines must be properly deployed or results will be disappointing. Manufacturing turtle set lines at home is reasonably easy.

Some critters, such as wild turtles, can be kept alive till needed for the table.

Ideally, use a 6/0 hook. I fully understand that most city survivors will have to use whatever fishhooks they have on hand or can trade for. More important than hook size, an 8-inch piece of wire leader should be placed between the hook and line. Turtles have tough, sharp beaks. They quickly gnaw through any non-metallic line.

Baited setlines can be attached to floating plastic bottles, overhanging branches or roots, though floating bottles may be too obvious. It is very important to keep any turtle bait well up off the bottom and 1 to 2 feet below the surface of the water. This is a very important concept. Don't use a long line—simply throw it out into a pool on the bottom. Baits held relatively near the surface won't attract crayfish and it might possibly catch a larger fish rather than a turtle. Turtles hooked near the surface on short lines cannot tangle and hide easily.

The hook should be baited with a solid chunk of muscle or gristle. Fat, skin, and feathers are not good baits. Piles of roadkill often make excellent hook bait.

Keep turtles alive till needed for the pot. They keep in water-filled barrels, tubs, or small cages, but the very best way to keep them is by drilling a small hole in the shell edge and attaching a long wire. Simply throw the turtle back into the lake, tethering it

FOOD

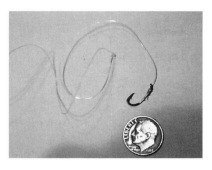

Turtle and bird hook lines. Note the fine line and small hook on the bird model, left, and the steel wire on the turtle line, right.

by wire to a stake, root, or branch. They live and eat on their own and may even fatten a bit.

Other Aquatic Food Sources

Many other critters of interest to hungry city survivors are found near or in water. Crayfish and minnows are not much, but are something. They can be caught in small fish traps.

Muskrats live in water. They are excellent eating, tasting much like very lean duck or goose. The easiest way to catch them is to place a fish trap with a 3- to 4-inch cone in front of an underwater muskrat burrow. They swim out into the trap and are caught.

Frogs are good eating but I don't know of an energy-efficient method of collection unless it is with a powerful flashlight and spear at night. This method may not practical or possible in many areas.

Ducks and geese often frequent ponds, lakes, and rivers. They can be caught in a variety of traps. The easiest way is to place a tiny hook or a thin piece of light fishing line baited with a single kernel of corn or wheat. This gets them about as easily and often as virtually any other method.

SNARES

Other than water critters, many other different animals that could advantageously end up in the pot are available in the city. Cats and dogs are some of these!

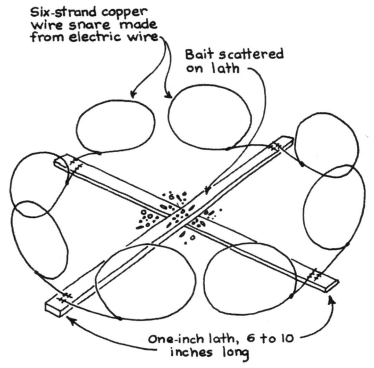

The African bird snare.

For some unexplained reason, some cities have many more dogs than cats and vice versa. Both critters are fairly easy to trap using snares in places they commonly run. They can also be taken with silenced .22 rifles when the opportunity is there. Carry your gun and shoot them when you see them; don't go out hunting.

Snares are a kind of wire lasso into which critters push themselves resulting in their capture. Pushing into a snare is fairly natural for wild critters that move around through tight holes, under fences, or through openings in buildings. Professional snares have one-way locks that prevent the cable from loosening.

Ideally, city survivors will have a few snares in their tool kit. If not, snares can be made from light wire. A man living in a western suburb of Chicago caught two marauding beavers by using homemade soft copper-wire snares the first time he ever tried.

FOOD

Out in the wild, rabbits are often snared with nylon cord or shoelaces. Readers who wish to purchase the real thing similar to ones pictured can write Neil or Rhonda Bock at The Snare Shop, 13191 Phoenix Avenue, Carroll, IA, 51401. The cost, complete, is about $1 per snare delivered in dozen lots.

Snares have been used to catch every animal on earth. Longtime readers are aware of my exploits using snares on moose, deer, and bear. Snares often strangle critters, especially those set to catch by the neck. Leghold snares are also reasonably easy, but not as easy at catching critters about the neck as they push through brush and grass.

Check snares at least once every day unless many critters start falling victim; then check more often. Unless set by experienced trappers, baits are seldom used. Set snares with an 8-inch loop from 12 to 14 inches off the ground for dogs. Smaller critters like cats are caught with smaller loops set closer to the ground.

RAT TRAPS

To city survivors, rats are an absolute bonanza. It is impossible to deplete or hinder a large, active colony even by taking as many as three or four 1-pound critters per week. Six to 12 young are born every 30 days to females, which rebreed 4 or 5 days after giving birth. Females start bearing at four to six months. Rats thrive on virtually any food, including power cables, feed bags, paper, nutshells, fruits, vegetables, or anything else of cellulose they can get a tooth into.

A slick colony trap can be constructed out of a 55- or 30-gallon steel barrel. Rig a smooth board or length of slick aluminum on a hinge on the barrel so that the board or metal extends to the ground but is carefully balanced at the top. Construct it so that a 12-ounce weight on the end over the barrel tips the beam into the barrel, dumping Mr. Rat inside.

Rub a very small amount of cheese or meat onto the end of the balance arm. Rats that walk from the floor up onto the barrel on the balance arm are tipped, screeching and scratching, into the smooth-sided barrel. Empty the barrel twice a day or they will eat each other.

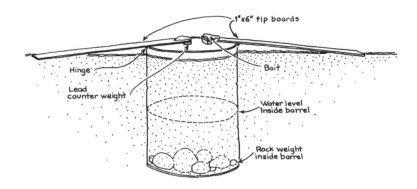

Colony traps are useful for live-trapping many critters.

The first trapped rat will call others to come have a look. These traps must be set in among colonies of rats. At times, larger barrels must be dug into the ground a bit; otherwise the balance arms, which must reach the ground, are too long to balance correctly.

Rats can also be caught in small cage-type live traps set in their runs or with bait near the run. Commercial cage traps are available, or you can simply make a little cage trap out of 1/2-inch hardware cloth with a front door that only swings inward as the rat pushes on it to get to the bait.

Snaring rats with very light cable is practical, but you gotta be very hungry. Make snares out of six or eight hair-thin wires pulled from an appliance cord. Loops are set about 1 1/2 inches in diameter in rat runs. Set out eight or 10 snares at a time. After sufficient rats are caught, pull the snares for a week.

Ductile copper acts as its own irreversible slipknot. Hung up, rats quickly strangle themselves, explaining why the traps should be set out in large numbers and checked frequently, and why this is such a disgusting procedure. Even I question regularly eating strangled rat!

BIRDS

There are a few edible birds in cities. Especially cities with older

FOOD

buildings, damaged and opened so that roosts are convenient. There are pigeons, seagulls, starlings, and even an occasional robin or thrush. Birds are good food for survivors when they can be caught without great effort. Birds fly out to get their own food and water without outside help or direction. The been there, done that folks tell me my large flight traps as described in *Survival Poaching* and *Live Off the Land in the City and Country* are impractical for real hard-core city survival. Too big, obvious, tough to build, and too tough to move, they say.

One effective method, previously mentioned for ducks and geese, is to bait very small fishhooks tied to light fishing line with single kernels of corn, a pea, or grain of wheat. Fishhooks can be set unobtrusively in large numbers on building tops in parks or wherever birds feed and where hooking them will not attract attention.

African bird snares are a practical, efficient alternative to larger, cumbersome, obvious bird traps. African bird snares perform nicely on all birds from sparrow size up through turkeys. Snare sizes must be adjusted, but realistically there are only three: small for robins; intermediate for pheasants, grouse, and ducks; and larger sizes for turkeys and geese.

These snare assemblies are made from cross-strips of flat wood. Simple laths, pickets, or even paint can stirrers will work for little snare assemblies. Two-by-four limbs or pieces of wood make a good basis for goose and turkey snares.

Small, hair-thin wires are pulled from copper-wire appliance cord for the snares themselves. Each device has four snares, one on each arm of the wooden cross. Use five or six strands of wire for little birds and 10 or 12 strands on larger critters.

Bait is placed in the middle of the cross. Birds that come in to eat quickly get their legs or necks caught in the snare. Loss of the device is sometimes a problem. Even very small birds can pull the snare assembly out of sight in rough, rubbly areas.

Other, much more complex bird-catching devices are out there, but hooks and African bird snares will virtually always do the job without a great deal of stumbling around.

Cattails growing in the upper Amazon Valley in eastern Ecuador. Cattail plants grow everywhere.

CATTAILS

Absolutely every city in the world I know of has cattails growing someplace within its boundaries. I have observed them from Barrow, Alaska, to Washington, D.C., to Quito, Ecuador.

Cattails were real manna for our Indians. They specifically camped near large cattail beds so they could feed off the plants. Cattails are always nutritious and healthy, even when grown in heavily polluted waters. There's no question about their identity. They are the ones with brown, tufty, wiener-like flowers at the end of a long stem that we used to dip in diesel and burn for torches when we were kids. It is impossible to mistake these guys for something else.

Cattails as a source of food have so many ways of treating you, you are bound to like one of them. Starting at first blush of spring, shoots grow up from the main roots that eventually become this year's stem and leaves. These fresh, new little shoots are good eat-

FOOD

Springtime brings new cattail shoots, which are good eating.

Cattail roots can be dug in fall and winter. With a rabbit or muskrat thrown in the pot, whole families have survived the winter on boiled cattail.

When fresh food is at a premium, cattails offer an easy-to-find solution.

ing. Dig and cut up these shoots when they are about 4 to 10 inches long. After 10 inches, the shoots start getting stringy and tough, with a kind of bitter taste, but they still can be harvested, steam-cooked, and eaten up until the plants are about 18 inches tall.

Cut the young shoots into macaroni-sized chunks. Boil or steam. They are best with salt and butter, but these seasonings probably won't be available in survival circumstances. Reportedly they are nutritious. These shoots can also be canned, frozen, or pickled, much like asparagus. When the main season is on, production from just a small patch can be surprisingly large.

Next comes a harvest from the flowers. These are the dry, brown wiener-shaped tops that all of us have seen in cattail patches. Before maturing, these flowers are green, tender, and good, much like ears of corn. Pick them as early as possible. Steam in a flat, covered pan for about 15 minutes.

Shortly after the flowers mature, they pollinate. We often see clouds of yellow dust flying about bodies of water without knowing the pollen is from the cattails. This pollen ranges from edible to quite good. Collect it by placing a thin plastic bag over the flower and shaking vigorously. Usually a teaspoon of pollen will be harvested per plant.

Use this pollen half-and-half with wheat flour or use it straight just like flour. The resulting biscuits are heavy, filling, and hard. Some people say they may even be as nutritious as biscuits made with flour. Realistically, I have no way of measuring this nutrition.

Cattail roots actually fatten up in anticipation of winter's lean times. During fall and winter these roots are dug up, cleaned, and cut up to be boiled and eaten. Eat the whole porridge-like mess or filter and dry the starch from the fiber as a kind of super-bland mashed-potato mix. Entire families have lived through winters on these roots with only addition of a small rabbit, a rat or—in some cases—a muskrat to the pot. Don't mistake this for good, but it is life-sustaining. All survival food is monotonous.

Exercise care with winter harvest of cattails. The bed will be slowly killed by removal of the roots.

CITY GARDENS

There are common edible items that city survivor hunter/gatherers can expect to find and use to augment their food supplies in or near built-up areas. All will definitely not be available all of the time. When available, all are relatively quick and easy, nicely meeting survival-thermodynamics criteria. Cattails are the exception, in that they are always available in some form or another. In spite of my best efforts to call attention to their value as emergency food, few survivors seem to know or care about cattails.

Gardens are possible even in the most intense inner city situations. Even in the heart of the asphalt jungle, gardens can be eked out of vacant lots, along boulevards, in grassy median strips along superhighways, and in highway cloverleaf structures. I have even seen nice rooftop gardens in downtown Rome and Chicago. These gardens raised ornamental plants, but could easily have contained something as practical as beans, zucchini, carrots, and potatoes.

Available water seems to be the limiting factor in cities, much more than locating a patch of suitable topsoil.

Theft from one's survival garden in the city was a concern for me, personally. Out in the country garden theft is common. "Not to worry," the been there, done that committee says. "Most inner city people don't know a green bean from an edible pod pea," they say. "(The) average city slicker will know large, typical vegetables, such a pumpkins and carrots, tended in neat, orderly, weed-free rows. But they fail miserably to recognize carrots or potatoes growing randomly in the ground."

City survival gardeners require very fast-growing, high-yield garden vegetables that average people won't recognize growing out in what seems like the wild. That these vegetables are also easy to process and are nutritious is another bonus. These are the garden items experts always suggest: potatoes, green beans, carrots, and zucchini.

Potatoes just barely made the list. Even though they produce more food per unit of land than any other crop on earth, they are relatively difficult to grow and store. Raising successive crops of potatoes on the same ground is a sure formula for devolution into nothing yields.

A multitude of fungal and bacterial diseases limit amateur potato production. Successfully keeping potato tubers for seed over the winter is never easy. Anyone who has ever kept spuds under the sink knows that even treated, commercial potatoes sprout and spoil easily. Potatoes are a 120-day crop in the northern hemisphere. They should be started as soon as the soil temperature reaches 54 degrees.

Potato tops are not good for anything except nourishing and supporting the tubers below. Few people will actually recognize a potato plant growing out by itself. Plant seed pieces about 4 inches deep. Sprouting occurs within 3 weeks. Soil should be mounded up around the plants to give the spuds more room in which to grow.

Carrots yield well, and they are fairly easy to raise and store. In most cases, mature carrots are simply left in the ground over the winter. Cover with 6 inches of leaves, grass, and duff. Dig up as needed for the pot.

The devil with carrots is getting the seed sprouted in the spring. Their minuscule seeds are easily buried too deep and lost. I cover cover the seeds with a light layer of peat moss and a piece of heavy canvas for 10 days to give them a chance to warm and sprout.

This leaves green beans and zucchini. Beans are excellent for city survivors because the mature pods can be left to dry on the plant when there are too many green beans to be otherwise processed. Production of food from 200 bean plants can be prodigious. Beans manufacture their own nitrogen fertilizer. Seeds saved from the last crop are always viable. When finally induced to sprout, beans do well on even very tired, poor soil.

Most zucchini are also open-pollinating, meaning seeds can be kept from one year to the next. Zucchini are a very short-term crop; it only takes around 53 days from planting to harvesting mature fruit. Everyone knows about the production ability of zucchini. In many places it is the subject of jokes. The biggest problem is storage; zucchini can be kept fresh for about 60 days, but after that they get moldy and deteriorate. Long-term storage entails freezing or canning.

All gardening, city or country, requires practice. Learning curves can be steep, but no two areas in the world are exactly the same relative to gardening techniques. City residents who believe they might someday become survivors can easily learn by placing a few hills of beans, zucchini, and potatoes out in the flower patch for practice. Few seeds and little space are required to experiment. Knowledge gained will be invaluable, especially when spread over

FOOD

a whole lifetime. Small-scale fooling around with garden vegetables leads to a continued supply of fresh seeds at the retreat.

I raised beans, carrots, and zucchini experimentally in a small plot across the street from a condo in which I lived in Boise, Idaho. There was abundant space in the lawns and flower beds among the high-rise buildings. But these flower beds were well tended and I risked having my little experimental garden mistaken for weeds and pulled up. Across the street I noticed a landowner who never mowed, pulled weeds, or fussed in any fashion with his yard. I planted there during the dark of night—just a batch of seeds to see what would happen.

Nobody expects very much activity on the part of greenskeepers or gardeners during a city's collapse. No doubt, concerns about errant weeding would not be justified if everything else around has turned to worms. My experimental seeds sprouted and grew, but languished when I was unable to water them. Boise receives only 7 inches of rain per year, on average—it's really a desert.

City survivors could successfully learn hunting and gathering techniques on the job. They could also learn to garden in 3 to 4 years. By then, the emergency will have passed or you will have died of starvation.

RAISING LIVESTOCK

Livestock can be successfully raised in the deep inner city.

Eight-week-old rabbits will be butchered in about 2 more weeks when they weigh 3 pounds.

Chickens and other domestic animals can be raised by city survivors.

Third-worlders do it all the time. It is generally small livestock, with goats being the largest. But, as with all animals, they are made of meat and will sustain life. My father raised rabbits and pigeons for 3 years; it was his and his brother's duty to keep the critters alive. This is probably more responsibility than most 12-year-olds in our society could assume.

Small animal pens and nest boxes are stored against the time of need by the city survivor.

Rabbits

As mentioned earlier, three doe rabbits and a buck will produce sufficient young that survivors can count on at least two rabbit meals per week. Figure a litter of six to eight young weighing 3 pounds every 8 weeks

Common pigeons are the perfect livestock for city survivors—they are prolific, hardy, and fly out to find their own food and water.

throughout the year. Dad claimed he rebred their does 4 days after they gave birth. The does then started production of the next litter while still nursing the first litter. I never wanted to crowd my rabbits that much, but dad pointed out that this is the way it happens all by itself out in nature.

Rabbit hutches are roughly 20-x-18-x-30 inches deep, made of 1/2-inch chicken wire top and sides. The bottom is made of 1/2- x-1-inch hardware cloth. Rabbits produce huge quantities of compost, which is useful in the garden. All this must fall through the hardware cloth on the bottom. Does like having a nest box, about 1 foot on a side and 18 inches deep. Cut a 4-inch access hole in front. The top should be hinged to open for inspection. Each buck and doe should have a hutch, plus one extra hutch per litter to keep them from weaning for 10 weeks, when they are butchered. Any older and they start breeding among themselves as well as consuming huge amounts of food, with little additional size gain to show for it.Figure one nest box per doe. The buck doesn't need one.

Bean stalks, leaves, hay, grass, cornstalks, zucchini rinds, carrot tops, and any other cellulose material can be gathered as feed for rabbits. During spring, summer, and fall they can be fenced into small grassy areas to eat on their own. Summer and fall are also the times when grass and weeds are cut, cured in the sun and then piled for winter food. I also recommend storing a bit of commercial feed against the time when the home-produced kind runs short. Don't try running rabbits out in areas where hungry soldiers, owls, or dogs are likely to find them.

Rabbits are easy, but not really easy to raise. Now and then, especially in the winter, domestic rabbits fail to breed or lose their litters. There's no obvious explanation, the litter is just born dead or quickly weakens and dies. Often it is the doe's fault. I give her two chances and then off to the pot.

Pigeons

Semidomestic pigeons are another kind of livestock city survivors can use to great advantage. Once established, pigeons mostly care for themselves. They need a protected, secluded roosting area more than a pen. Pigeons fly in and out for their own food and water. They pair for life, producing eight pairs of young per year, always setting two eggs. The young weigh almost a pound dressed at maturity in 30 days.

Fifteen pairs of pigeons produce enough young that, at a minimum, city survivors can figure on four pigeons for dinner per week. Theoretically it should be more than that, but things seldom work out perfectly. The process of producing young is materially speeded by a biological oddity of pigeons. Males take over the chore of raising the young from about day 26 till first flight, while she starts the next two-egg nest.

On the downside, pigeons are extremely dirty and full of parasites. They reportedly carry virtually every disease and parasite known to man. They are smelly and pigeon whitewash is, of course, not particularly aesthetic. Nevertheless, these critters turn themselves into lots of food. Fifty years ago, raising squabs for market was big business in the United States. Poultry factories have reduced the enterprise to the little we see today.

Here is how to start a city survival pigeon enterprise:

Select a high room or attic in a building in the city onto which pigeons can easily fly. An attic loft with a window end that can be opened is ideal. For aesthetic and health reasons, it is best if this pigeon loft is as far from living quarters as possible. Pigeons really smell bad on hot, humid summer evenings and they make a surprising amount of noise. Nail or screw a number of flat boards on which the pigeons can roost and eventually build their own nests. It is best if the roost has a sound roof and enough windows to provide light. Rats prey on pigeons, so be sure to protect the birds from these critters.

Breeding stock is acquired by using small snares or a flashlight and net at night to catch roosting pigeons. Collect 10 or 12 pairs to transfer to your loft. Pigeons reach breeding maturity within 3 to 5 months, but this may take too long, especially if the enterprise is launched after turmoil comes. Catching more pairs now rather than less obviously gets the enterprise off to a speedier start. The breeding life of a pair of pigeons is about 5 years.

New captives must be held till they lose their previous homing instinct (as in homing pigeons) or till you can take this instinct away. Tightly coop new pigeons in their new loft. Even though feed can be costly and difficult to find, give them all they will eat for 15 days. At the same time, hang a very powerful permanent magnet over the feed pan not too far from the eating pigeon's heads. Take the magnet away after 8 days. On day 15, open the roost access window during the night, so the critters can leave first thing in the morning. Usually they return!

Previously wild pigeons kept cooped longer than 15 days start going downhill physically. Expect high mortality in these circumstances if they must be kept locked up.

When food and water are abundantly available out in nature for the released birds, pairs will start nesting almost immediately.

Summarily eat any singles that show no sign of pairing and nesting. These will be really tough but they make OK soups.

Incubation takes about 18 days. The two eggs hatch surprisingly close together. After hatching, young pigeons seem to double in size weekly. At 28–30 days the young reach maximum size and should be butchered before their first flight.

Pigeons are easily roasted, and taste somewhat similar to chicken. Roasting is OK when birds are super abundant but most survivors are best served by spreading the protein around a bit. This entails making these guys into potpies, soups, or stews.

Goats, Chickens, and Ducks

At one time, great numbers of goats seemingly running wild lived a few blocks from downtown Beirut. It seems that they actually belonged to someone: several times a month, the owners crept out to shoot a kid or two for the pot. The goats' utility was that they mostly took care of themselves, eating virtually anything made of plant material. On the other hand, theft from the herd may have been a problem. Whether Americans could handle goats is questionable. I recently tried to find a goat to butcher and eat for a dinner for some African friends. Goat owners I talked to reacted in absolute horror at the thought of someone actually eating one of their pet goats.

I personally have raised many chickens, ducks, and goats within the centers of fairly large cities. In my opinion, they are not sufficiently easy, prolific, or disease-free enough to warrant inclusion in city survival livestock. Chickens and ducks are really tough to get to nest on any reliable year-round schedule. They require huge amounts of often tough-to-provide feed.

Their one element of charm involves the fact that chickens and ducks can be kept alive in a kind of live-storage situation.

STORAGE

Food storage and barter are also valid components of a successful city survival food program. Most city survivors emphasize this component over all others. It is a concern that too many survivors will take what presently seems like the quick, easy approach, making food storage their only survival food option. Since we never know with certainty how long any crisis will last, some sort of food replacement strategy will always have to be part of an entire program. Unfortunately storage is not only easy, it leaves a false impression that something has actually been done.

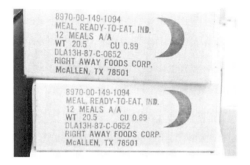

Stored food such as these MREs are only part of a survival food program.

The continuing admonition of this book is to start now, even on a very modest scale, to learn how to garden, hunt and gather, and raise edible livestock. We can't simply store huge quantities of food and allow events to overtake us.

Even under ideal conditions, when little or no prior planning is made to begin consuming stored food, stockpiles will gradually start to diminish as they are used a little bit at a time to support foods coming in from the garden, field, rabbit hutch, and pigeon loft.

But how much food do city survivors need to store? The rule of thumb is that humans will require between 1 and 1 1/2 pounds of dehydrated protein, carbohydrates, and calories on a dry-matter basis per day. A second rule of thumb suggests that bland, monotonous foods that survivors in their initial doldrums and boredom are not tempted to sit around and eat should be stored. In other words, you won't be tempted to sit around eating if the groceries are monotonous.

This psychology may preclude use of some more traditional survival foods. Various plans—including army surplus MREs (meals, ready to eat), cases and cases of bully beef, and peas, dried, dehydrated, etc.—have all been put forward as survival food plans. I, too, have *some* MREs as well as dehydrated food in storage. But these are expensive and of limited value. I still much prefer more basic, common boring commodities, which are cheap, easy, and convenient. There's no need to send across the country when you can get them at the local grocery.

Whole grains such as whole wheat, barley, and untreated dried peas are too basic, in my opinion. Wheat and barley, as they come from the farm, are very inexpensive and easy to acquire. But, if they come directly from the farm they will also contain dirt, trash, chaff, rodent droppings, and bugs that are not particularly nice to deal with in our food. Also, this stuff is the devil to store over the long term.

Avoid all of the instruction regarding dry ice, freezing, and whatnot by purchasing commodities that have been factory cleaned, sterilized, and packaged. To that end I really like dried split peas, dried milk, lentils, dried beans, milled wheat flour, basic sugar, and vegetable oil as stored survival rations.

Dried split peas, lentils, and dried beans are, to some extent, an acquired taste. Especially if that's all there is with little variety day to day. But add a bit of rabbit, pigeon, cattail, fish, duck, or rat from time to time and these foods start tasting good. They are also extremely nutritious.

All these dried goods are simple and cheap to purchase as well as easy to store. Absolutely every large warehouse supermarket I have been in has all of these items in large, durable, sealed bags.

My basic supply for a family of four for 1 year, assuming some augmentation from fields and garden, is as follows:

- Five 50 pound sacks of sugar: about $60
- Six 50 pound sacks of flour: about $48
- Ten 25 pound sacks of cleaned, treated lentils: about $75
- Ten 25 pound sacks of split peas: about $60
- Ten 25 pound sacks of dried beans: about $70
- Two 3 gallon jugs of vegetable oil: about $24
- 100 pounds of dried milk: about $200
  Total: about $537

Try buying this level of eating using MREs for anywhere near this money.

Reconstituted with water and bulked with a few other items brought into the retreat, the above stocks will definitely sustain life for a party of four for 1 year. Simplicity always counts heavily in survival situations, and this inventory is simplicity itself. The entire year's supply will fit under a folding table!

As long as the bags are kept from dampness, rats and mice, bugs, and physical damage, all this supply can be stacked as is on shelves. I presently keep two-thirds of my supply piled on an open shelf in a special, mouse-proofed storeroom.

Most city survivors take the additional precaution of further sealing their emergency rations in large plastic garbage cans. Although rotating supplies is advised, I have peas and lentils sealed in these cans from 1976! All are in reasonably good condition, with little to no stale taste when cooked up.

Barter of excess or unneeded food supplies is mentioned by all of the been there, done that crew. Because this list of emergency foods is so modest and currently so cheap and easy, survivors may wish to double or triple listed amounts. Storage and caching involves more than this humble list of food, and will be covered in depth in Chapter 9.

A MATTER OF TASTE

Many of these food items are very much an acquired taste. It is likely you won't like lentils. Most Americans do not. Experimenting a bit now could make the process easier later. In their defense, lentils are considered to be one of the best, most nutritious high-density sources of vegetable protein!

This chapter is about sustaining life on a number of unusual to weird to frequently repulsive food items. Not a lot of familiar meat and potato items are found here. My mind goes back to the Indians (on the Indian subcontinent) as contrasted with the Chinese whenever I contemplate food issues and survival. Both countries have roughly similar land areas, population densities, growing seasons, soil, rainfall, and general crop-raising capacities.

Yet there are dramatic differences in their societies. At the same time that the Indians go hungry, sometimes starving as a result of periodic famine, the Chinese grow fat. The question is, "Why?" It's simplicity itself. My personal, on-the-ground observation is that the

FOOD

Chinese eat everything from shark fins to bird nests, to duck feet and tongues, convincing themselves in the process that they are eating delicacies.

Indians, on the other hand, are beset and constrained by dozens and dozens of cultural, religious, social, and structural taboos that preclude them from enjoying and eating things all around them. Indians of some sort or another won't eat pork, cattle, chickens, snakes, some seafood, some mammals, and a host of stuff in between. An average Indian hotel restaurant usually has five different menus, virtually from five different kitchens requiring five different sets of pots and pans. How they traditionally sorted it out without using computers is a mystery. The problems with confusion and inefficiencies in this system are obvious.

Survivors, in the city or anyplace else, don't have time for such fooling around. You will have to eat what is on hand, receiving with thanks whatever will sustain life.

Chapter 7

Survival Food Preservation

Quick, why do commercial potato farmers often leave the equivalent of fifty 100-pound bags of potatoes per acre lying in the field to waste? Fully understanding this concept is central to understanding the means and necessity of survival food preservation.

No matter if it is a tiny city survivor's garden plot or a 40,000-acre Iowa corn farm, edible food matures and comes rushing in over a very short time span. Harvest doesn't happen all at once, but almost. Potato farmers, worried about 450-bags-to-the-acre yields, won't give a rip for tiny potatoes—worth, at most, a penny a pound—that fall through the sorting chain.

It's all a Golden Rule of Food Production, of which most long-term city residents are completely unaware: Provisions must be made, both in the survivor's thinking and his emergency supplies, to handle rush harvests. Nine times out of 10, harvests happen quickly, often under great duress. Think of it as suddenly being given a 1,200 pound steer that is only yours if you can process it. Also saying that temperatures are in the 90s adds realism to the example.

What are you going to do with the critter? Eat one or two steaks or a pound of burger? That would be nice, but it doesn't work that way. To eat one steak you either have to eat it all or figure some way to preserve the remainder. Russian quartermasters, for example, delivered live cattle to the soldiers on the Eastern Front during World War I as their daily food ration. Russian quartermasters didn't fuss with MREs. One cow reportedly was issued for every 600 soldiers. Soldiers butchered the critters right there on the front line and ate it all immediately.

One way, but probably not always the best way, of storing food is delaying butchering till the time of need or, in the case of vegetable gardens, delaying harvesting. Indeed, live fish can be left in the fish trap; turtles, as mentioned, can be wired up in deep holes in the river; pigeons can be left on the roost; and rabbits, to some limited extent, can be left in their hutch. Back on the farm we frequently butchered chickens when company came over unexpectedly. But that was chickens.

New potatoes dug, dried, and ready for storage.

Problem is, fish and turtles might contrive to escape; rabbits and pigeons grow older and tougher, eating lots of precious food in the process; and, of course, garden vegetables can easily rot on the vine or in the ground if they are not dealt with promptly. Theft is a serious problem in any high-energy survival situation. Leave too much largesse on display and others may recognize and appropriate it.

Adding shelf life to food is an ancient problem. Most techniques we currently have available came over on the Mayflower. The only exception is freezing and perhaps freeze-drying. Freezing is a viable survival technique in some circumstances, but generally we still rely

SURVIVAL FOOD PREPARATION

on salting, drying, and canning or some combination of the above. Preservation by canning really only came on the scene about 1795 during the time of Napoleon, who encouraged this new technology as a means of feeding his armies! Making jerky out of surplus meat is the oldest and perhaps least exotic food preservation technique. In a complete survival circumstance, it is often the only way of preserving our hypothetical 1,200-pound steer.

BUTCHERING ANIMALS

The most important thing to remember when faced with butchering an animal is this: don't panic. These directions are not as complicated as they first seem. Everything is actually pretty logical. But remember that the longer the animal has been dead the more complicated the process becomes, so try to begin butchering 10 to 15 minutes after it has been slaughtered. Starting at absolute ground zero for those who have never gutted and butchered a critter, here is how to proceed:

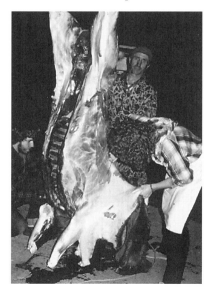

Roll it over on its back with legs skyward. Make a cut with your knife through the skin all the way from the base of the bottom lip straight down the middle to the bunghole. Nature

Skinning and halving a large elk

Halves of sheep after an all-day butchering session.

has placed a kind of line along the belly of most critters to follow when cutting.

Cut through the skin deep into the neck, exposing the critter's tough, rubbery, almost corrugated windpipe. Cut the head off, leaving as much of the neck as possible. Pull the windpipe free of the neck up to the brisket. Using a carpenter's saw, cut through the brisket, continuing straight down through the bottom of the rib cage.

Cut down to, but not into, the stomach and intestine area. Puncture of the gut or stomach is messy, but a thorough washing later can salvage the situation. General aesthetics and cleanliness are better served by not cutting into the guts. This becomes progressively more difficult the longer the critter is dead. Gases collect in the stomach, pressing it out against the wall of the critter.

Forcibly spread the two rib sides. Pull the windpipe, still attached to the heart and lungs, out of the carcass. Cutting around the diaphragm muscle separating the heart and lungs from the intestinal cavity will be necessary. Try to pull all—heart, liver, lungs, stomach, and intestines—clear of the carcass. Other than salvaging the heart and liver, most of this is left for the coyotes and birds. Notice we did not bleed the critter. By now it is obvious that quickly dressed animals will bleed profusely without special attention.

Feel for the Achilles tendon immediately up from the heel. Carefully poke your knife into the space between the tendon and the bone on each leg, making a hole into which you can put a hook. Be very careful not to cut the tendon. Hang the carcass up by its two hind legs. The legs should be spread-eagled and the carcass clear of the floor. Starting with a knife at the bunghole, cut along the top edge of the skin on each leg aiming toward the heel. Cut the skin clear around the leg just below the hook—again, be careful not to cut the tendon by which you are hanging the critter—and start cutting and peeling the skin away from the body. Done carefully, you should be able to do this without nicking either meat or skin. Leave as much fat and muscle on the carcass as possible. Experienced skinners—my wife included—do a cow, goat, deer, or horse in 10 minutes or less. First timers may take as much as an hour. Survivors are generally quick studies. Next time the process won't be so time consuming and bewildering.

SURVIVAL FOOD PREPARATION 103

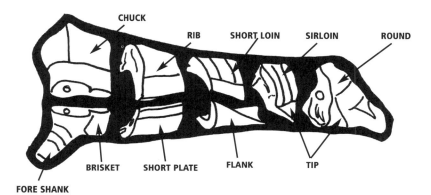

After skinning is complete, examine the inside of the carcass for anything that looks like guts that you may have missed the first time. Kidneys, especially, have a habit of hiding in the fat immediately under the ribs. Saw down the middle of the carcass from neck to bunghole along the backbone. Cut through the center of the bone, not the meat on either side of the backbone. Halving these critters is probably the most physically demanding part of the process, but necessary if they are to be chilled out properly. Wash the critter down, preferably with cold running water from a hose, if you have it available. This is particularly important if there were punctured guts or stomach. If you do not have access to running water, try hanging in the cold open air. In hot Africa, we hung meat overnight to chill, but had to eat it or jerk it the next day.

Cutting the critter up into much smaller "butcher shop"-sized pieces of meat is controversial. Everybody has his own way of doing it. Certainly I have butchered thousands of critters and I do not believe I have ever cut two out exactly the same. Wash down the floor at this point to deal with the debris and blood and keep the area tidy. The critter will continue to bleed some, but this blood on the wet floor can be dealt with later.

Look at the butcher-shop schematic above for ideas regarding various cuts of meat that can be taken from a halved carcass.

Everything down to goat- and dog-sized critters is handled in much the same fashion. Rabbits, cats, and rat-sized animals are much quicker and easier to process. I have often, for example, skinned and gutted five rabbits in 10 minutes. But I have been doing this work since I was 11.

Smaller animals are always skinned first and then stripped of entrails. Cut off the head unless it is a mink or coon-type critter for which the skin is saved. Hang it spread-eagled by the hind legs. Cut from the bung to the top of the legs, through the skin, along the top edge. Carefully cut and peel the skin down over the head in one great tube, resulting in what the trade calls a "case-skinned critter." Other methods are workable, but this one is as simple and easy for beginners as it gets.

The entrails are exposed and removed by cutting up from the top of the rib cage through the body wall to the bung. Simply strip everything out that looks like guts. Be certain to look up clear into the chest cavity for the heart and lungs. Left inside, they can quickly sour the meat.

How to dress poultry? Most neophyte survivors take the simple expedient of summarily pulling the weak skin from the bird by grasping and tugging on the attached feathers. Professionally, birds are almost always plucked, leaving the skin—which most people consider tasty and nutritious—intact. In my opinion, birds destined for the smokehouse are best left with the skin on.

Plucking is fairly easy when done correctly. Heat water to between 140 and 150 degrees for such birds as chickens, turkeys, quail, pheasant, and grouse, and between 160 and 170 degrees for ducks and geese. Add a small bit of detergent to the water to dissolve the oil in the feathers and allow the hot water to soak in. Time of dipping depends on the size of the bird, with a minute being about right for chickens. Swish the bird up and down, allowing the heat to penetrate to the skin. Test by pulling a few feathers. When the bird is perfectly dipped, the feathers will pull easily from the body and legs, though you will have to tug a bit on the long wing feathers. If the bird is dipped for too short a time, or if the water is not hot enough, the feathers will not come out. If the bird is dipped for too long, or if the water is too hot, the skin cooks and comes off with the feathers.

After plucking, singe off remaining hair-like feathers (pinfeathers) on the carcass. Cut a small hole in the rear of the

SURVIVAL FOOD PREPARATION

bird—two or three fingers for small birds and fist-size for larger birds—through which the entrails can be removed. Slide your fingers in over the top of the guts and pull the whole mass out in a lump, going back in to probe along the back ribs and up into the chest cavity to be sure you have all the pieces. Be careful of the bile sac on the liver—puncturing it will allow the green liquid to spill, souring the meat. Salvage the heart, liver, and gizzard. The bile sac can be cut or peeled away and thrown away with the guts. The easiest way to deal with the gizzard is just to cut off the two protruding ends where the meat is, taking care not to puncture the inner sac containing the stones, which is tossed with the guts. There is also a plump sac called the crop that is between the neck and the top of the chest cavity. If full, you can find it easily. Approach it from the neck when you retrieve the windpipe. If you are careful and don't puncture it, it all comes out in one neat piece; puncture it and you get seeds, grass, bugs, or whatever the critter was eating all over the meat. All birds have crops, although they are less well developed in ducks and geese. When pulling the windpipe, be sure to get the larynx.

First-timers are usually shocked and discouraged to discover how little edible meat remains of a once large, plump critter.

PRESERVING MEAT

Freezing meat and vegetables, even if a generator is required, is often the quickest, safest, easiest, and most nutritious method of preserving food.

Processing now depends on what prior preparations have been made and what tools and materials are in your inventory. The simplest way, of course, is to crank up the generator to power a freezer. But we already know there won't be sufficient generators for all city survivors.

Brining

Nutrition, quality, aesthetics, and versatility suffer to some extent, but red meat, poultry, and fish can be preserved in salt brine. Plastic wastebaskets are ideal as brine tanks. Almost everyone already has these.

Common rock salt (NaCl) is the staff of life of any primitive survival program. City survivors are also going to have to have lots of it in hand before the crisis hits. No reason not to stockpile salt, even in a 31st floor condo deep within a city. Salt is dirt cheap, it stores well, and doesn't easily go out of condition as long as the bags are kept intact and dry. If all else fails, salt will be a hugely valuable trade good.

Salt-curing meat and some vegetables is possible using plastic waste baskets and large quantities of salt.

Cut meat into 1 1/2 to 2-pound chunks before brining.

Using clean, filtered, purified water, mix up half a plastic wastebasket of salt and water of sufficient strength to float an egg or russet-type baking potato. Low-solid Red Pontiac potatoes will give a false reading. There's not enough salt in the water to preserve meat when using these as a gauge.

All dense beef, goat, and dog meat should be cut into 1 1/2- to

2-pound chunks. Larger chunks brine too slowly. Spoilage may occur inside, especially around bones. Professionals brine using a syringe-like tool to inject salt water into really large ham-sized pieces of meat.

Ground meat can be successfully kept in brine, but it does turn gray, fall apart, and degrade a bit. Later it can be filtered or skimmed out of the brine with a sieve or screen. The question is, are the results better in brining chunks of meat that are later ground into burger, or grinding first and then brining? Try it either way.

All brined meat tastes better if it is boiled in water and repeatedly rinsed. Brined burger must be repeatedly soaked to make it edible.

Fish, fowl, and even pork and beef are best brined and stored separately. Poultry, which are essentially hollow, can be brined without chunking or boning. Brine containers easily become heavy and unwieldy and should be placed in a cool, protected area out of the sun and away from dust and dirt. Properly brined meat easily keeps for 2 or 3 years.

Smoking

Light brining is a half-step toward preservation by smoking. It is unclear whether salt saturation or smoke penetration adds shelf life. At any rate, brining and smoking seem not to lead to long-term storage. Meat, heavily brined or smoked, in a fairly hot fire only seems to keep 2 or 3 months at best. Lightly brined and smoked meat may not keep at all—a week or 10 days in hot weather, maximum.

Smoking can be undertaken in virtually any closed container that will house a small heat source on which some chips of hickory or apple wood are placed. Kettle cookers, regular little steel smoker boxes, wooden boxes, old refrigerators, and even heavy cardboard boxes all have been used as smokers. The heat source can be a couple of pieces of charcoal, an old electric hot plate, or even an old electric oven. I have even seen a propane torch used as a heat source in a small smoker. The plan is to close off the oxygen supply in the smoker box drum, container, or whatever, producing lots of dense smoke without flame.

Here we want to penetrate the meat with as much smoke as

possible, using as little heat as possible. Cooking the meat is not desirable. If a thermometer is available, keep temperatures down around 140 degrees. If you don't have a thermometer, keep it comfortably warm, but not hot to the touch.

Personally I have spoiled lots of meat trying to keep it too long after smoking. In a nonsurvival circumstance, smoked meat can be stored in the refrigerator until consumed. The only way to know for sure in your climate is to experiment now while it's not life and death.

Mason jars, lids, and rings for home canning.

Canning

Canning meat in glass jars is a bit risky and time consuming, but certainly is possible. For about 200 years it was a preservation method of choice. But when meat is cooked insufficiently long in large batches, it can turn to poison in the oxygen-free environment inside of glass jars. There are several precautions that can be taken that minimize the risk. Unfortunately, they simultaneously degrade the quality of the meat.

A home canning pot sits on a small, portable propane stove. Canning can be done virtually anywhere as long as supplies of LP gas hold out.

SURVIVAL FOOD PREPARATION

A large propane cooker, canner pot, or pressure cooker, canning jars, lids, and an abundant supply of jar lid hold-down rings are required to can both meat and vegetables. Without prior positioning of these vital supplies, there is little reason to rely on this method of preservation. Extra lids, hold-down rings, and canning jars are very inexpensive. Thirty dollars buys several years' supply, but it will take at least $100 to purchase a 7-quart pressure cooker. Pressure cookers are also used to cook up old, tough, or otherwise inedible meat.

Home canning of fruits and some vegetables is relatively easy. Both meat and vegetables can be done in a regular water bath with an open kettle, though the results are speedier and more certain using a pressure cooker. Country people, who tend to process their own food, might already own a pressure cooker. For city survivors, ownership of a pressure cooker will be a pure buy-it-now-to-put-in-storage play.

Start by cutting all meat into chunks of 1 pound or less. Brown these pieces thoroughly in an open pan on the propane stove. Brown slowly for about 20 minutes, till all red and pink disappear from the meat. Stuff the piping-hot meat chunks into canning jars. Quart jars store a great deal more meat, but pints—especially without a pressure cooker—are quicker and easier to boil and are sterilized with greater certainty. Most survivors limit home meat canning to pint jars when they don't have a pressure cooker.

Add 1 teaspoon of salt to each meat-packed jar. All jars, reused or new, must be thoroughly washed clean and scalded to be sterile. Fill the jars entirely with boiling water, driving all air out. Ensuring proper sterilization requires that quarts of meat be boiled four hours in an open water bath or 1 1/2 hours in a pressure cooker. Pints can be boiled in the open for 3 1/2 hours in an open bath or for 1 hour in a pressure cooker. Obviously this will take lots of energy. Pressure cookers quickly pay for themselves in time and energy saved.

As a final precaution, all meat canned at home using an open water bath—not a pressure cooker—should be cooked in an open pan an additional 10 minutes after opening prior to serving. By now it is obvious why many city survivors plan to try to use a freezer of some sort to preserve their meat and vegetables. Freezing takes far less total energy in the long run, it keeps everything in a more appetizing and nutritious form, and it is much easier when time is at an incredible premium.

Vegetables not frozen quickly must be canned. Freezing is better because of the fewer supplies and energy required. Freezing and canning are similar in their initial stages. Here is how to freeze vegetables:

To freeze vegetables such as beans and peas, first pick, clean, and thoroughly wash them. Blanch them in boiling water for 10 minutes to stop the enzyme action. Cool blanched batches of vegetables for 5 minutes in running water and then spread thinly on cookie sheets or in shallow pans. Place the pans of vegetables in the freezer. After freezing, break individual pieces apart and pack them into plastic storage bags that are again placed in the freezer.

Canning vegetables begins in a similar fashion. Again, start by washing, but wash more thoroughly than with freezing. All errant garden dirt must be removed. Huge amounts of labor are required, so much that canning may never be practical for some hard-core city survivors.

Blanch cleaned vegetables at a rolling boil for 10 minutes. Do not cool as when vegetables are frozen. Place still piping-hot vegetables in quart canning jars. Pack the jars as tightly as possible, adding one teaspoon of salt and filling to the top with boiling water.

Process the jars in an open water bath for 4 hours at a rolling boil or in a pressure cooker 1 1/2 hours. All vegetables processed in an open water bath must be cooked 10 additional minutes in an open pan before serving. Most vegetables take on a pretty bedraggled look by the end of processing.

Successfully placing canning lids on jars takes practice. Break new lids apart and place them in a shallow pan of boiling water. Boil for 10 minutes. Wipe the rim of each filled canning jar with a clean (freshly washed), dampened cloth to remove debris and grease. Remove the lids one at a time from the boiling water and place firmly on canning jars. There are two sizes of lids, little and big. Big-mouthed jars are generally surplus mayonnaise jars or whatnot, which quickly break in service. Initially a generous supply of each size lid is required. Lids are not reusable.

SURVIVAL FOOD PREPARATION

Cinch the lids down firmly with brass retainer rings made expressly for this purpose. When the contents of the jar boils in the boiling water bath, all air in the jar will be driven out. On cooling, the lids draw down on the jars, sealing them.

Hanging

It is a very old-fashioned method, but fresh meat can be hung and preserved for several weeks to 2 months in cool to modestly cold climates. How cold? Cool enough that no bugs are out. Generally about 38 to 40 degrees, max.

Hang the halved carcasses in a cool, draft-free area away from traffic and warmth of the living area. Gritty, airborne dust on the meat is not particularly nice. Throw a light bedsheet-weight cover on hanging meat to keep it clean.

In about 10 days the meat will become discolored to a very deep red or even maroon. Surface mold will form. Neither of these harms the edibility of the meat in the least. Toward the last the meat may even start to smell a bit. It's OK, but just hurry up with the eating, freezing, or drying before it gets much worse.

Will city survivors have a place to hang meat? Maybe out on a porch or balcony. Experience indicates that life will get extremely cramped in some apartments. It will definitely not be like the normal routines we currently enjoy. Hanging meat may not be possible, but it won't even be an option if you don't know about the method.

Jerking

Outside of freezing, jerking meat is certainly the simplest, easiest, safest, and perhaps most nutritious method of adding shelf life to very perishable products. This fact was dramatically brought home to me while watching allegedly primitive rural Africans quickly, easily process as many as four 400- to 500-pound critters per day into dried meat. They called it *biltong*. Performance of this wondrous deed was done without equipment or supplies. Butcher knives and a wild thorn bush rack were their most sophisticated equipment.

Little or no difference exists between jerky and biltong, except that the latter tends to be made from ostrich, oryx, or giraffe meat.

Rural Africans produce their jerky by hanging sliced pieces of meat on a thorn bush out in the direct sun in places where dust is minimal and gentle winds blow. The rule to follow in making jerky is that although use of some modern accouterments adds to processing efficiencies and perhaps aesthetics, only heat and air movement are really necessary to produce a nutritious, delicious, satisfactory product.

Marinating jerky meat isn't entirely necessary, but most survivors pretreat their surplus meat before starting the actual jerking process. These homemade marinating concoctions range from powdering with fine-ground pepper to soaking in a water, pepper, and salt mixture, to using Worcestershire sauce to using plain old honey and pepper.

Some folks don't like any of these, and fortunately these are not a requirement for good jerky. Others enjoy the peppery, salty taste these condiments carry into the meat.

We do know that fine-ground pepper and salt soaked into jerky both adds taste and reduces the chore of keeping pesky blowflies at bay till heat levels rise and the meat is sufficiently dry to avoid being fly-blown. Under nonemergency conditions, similar results can be achieved by starting the jerky out for a few minutes in a microwave. Or the entire job can be done on a kitchen range. By whatever source of heat, be cautious that the process proceeds sufficiently slowly that the meat dries rather than cooks.

Sanitation, always a problem when producing jerky, is better accomplished by working in the kitchen. Some natural gas and bottled gas ranges or burners may be operational, but it's best not to count on these in a real nitty-gritty survival situation.

Unless it is summer in northern latitudes or winter in southern Texas or Arizona, outdoor temperatures will not be suitable for natural jerky production. No problem! Large quantities of excellent jerky have been made around an open fire with snow on the surrounding ground. It would have seemed easier working on the ground level, but some survivors in Kuwait City and in Beirut cracked the concrete in their high-rise apartments when they built open fires on the bare cement floor. If it comes to that, find an old steel sheet, car fender, or whatever to protect the floor.

SURVIVAL FOOD PREPARATION

DRYING OR SMOKING RACK MADE FROM BEDSPRINGS

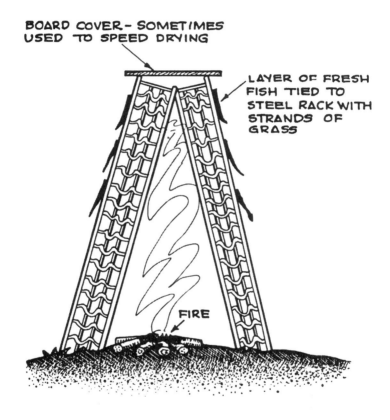

They are gone now, but at one time we shared the use of a set of two old steel bedsprings. Frequently we erected these in an inverted V over an open fire forming a kind of reusable drying rack. A rack could have been built out of wood, but the bedsprings were slick and easy.

Over the years, hundreds of pounds of fish, ducks, rabbits, and pheasants, as well as deer, elk, and moose meat were processed over these makeshift racks. City survivors will probably cure rat, cat, dog, and perhaps fish, geese, ducks, and pigeons on their racks. Something similar could be scroungeable in almost any city.

Believe it or not, tough, old, wild fat-free meat makes the best jerky. Far better than fatty, marbled, store-bought steaks or meat of virtually any kind. Any fatty, greasy meat, other than some fish, produces a sticky, rancid, foul-tasting, smelly end product. Fatty fish should be smoked or dried rather than jerked. Generally, fish such as carp, suckers, Kokanee, and dog salmon turn out OK to pretty good when smoked.

Cut meat into thin strips before jerking.

Commence the jerky enterprise by cutting thin, lean strips of meat from large cuts taken from the whole carcass. Meat bound for the jerky rack should be sliced no more than 1/2-inch thick. This is a time consuming and often difficult task. Slice across the grain, or at a minimum on the bias across the muscle. Otherwise the finished product may end up tougher than old wang leather.

Plain old charcoal-fired kettle-type barbecue pots or even gas grills work well to jerk meat. Place only three to five live briquettes in the grill. Set gas fires as low as possible. Open all vents, especially in the cover, so that heat from the fire circulates dry, fresh air into the kettle while simultaneously pushing moisture laden air out the top.

Recall again that jerky requires small, gentle heat and air movement. Temperatures of about 175 degrees are about right for those with both thermometer and a by-the-book approach to jerky making.

SURVIVAL FOOD PREPARATION

Meat can be jerked on common kettle-type barbecue grills or even over an open fire.

All jerky will eventually spoil. Insufficiently jerked jerky will spoil more quickly. Last fall we lost several pounds of jerky taken from freezer to refrigerator where we promptly forgot about it. Deterioration was delayed, but eventually it all went badly moldy and stank.

Test jerky as it dries. Properly dried jerky bends nicely before breaking. Cool a piece a bit, and then break it to see how dry it really is. Proper jerky bends to about 90 degrees, then breaks cleanly.

Effective drying takes about 24 to 48 hours over an open fire or out in a bright, hot sun. Kettle barbecues require 6 to 8 hours. Marinating in a brine-and-pepper solution definitely retards spoilage if eating all this extra salt and pepper is otherwise OK. Overjerking is always better than underjerking when longer term storage is an issue.

Finished, jerked meat has lost about two-thirds of its original volume and weight. Although in our society it is seldom used for such, jerky is wonderful reconstituted in soups and stews.

I have very occasionally gone further and made pemmican. Pemmican is an entirely different food. Generally, modern Americans do not appreciate the fatty, lardy mouth feel and taste.

Pemmican is assembled from 50 percent fine-chopped jerky, 25 percent crushed berries or fruit, and 25 percent lard or beef tallow. Maybe we will need a shot of calories such as this, but I wonder.

Dehydrating fruits and vegetables is very energy-efficient, leading to a high-quality, nutritious product.

Drying

As mentioned earlier, fish are really dried, not jerked. Use the same heated air circulation system as before, but brine longer with a slightly stronger solution. Dry longer and more thoroughly. Ugly, twisted, almost cardboard-tough fish are probably just about right.

Fruits such as apples, apricots, pears, plums, and peaches can also be dried successfully. Either a commercial drying rack or one made from common bug screen and small pieces of lumber will dry fruit. Processing for the dryer starts with slicing everything into pieces not more than a 1/2-inch thick. Then wash the pieces in a solution of 2 ounces of bleach per gallon of water.

Place treated pieces on the screen or dehydrator rack. Several layers of screen through which warm air is forced are usually most efficient. Again, it needn't be much heat, but movement of heat and air through the rack must occur. Drying takes from 6 to 12 hours. Rotating the pieces on the racks will speed things along a bit. Arrange so the driest are always on top. Properly dried fruit is tough but still a bit malleable. I am told that only 5 percent of food value is lost when drying fruits and vegetables.

The question is, will city survivors have access to sufficient quantities of fruits and perhaps vegetables to make drying feasible? And will there be screen racks and gentle heat needed to accomplish this enterprise? Very few cities in the United States have any fruit trees in their public areas. Too much mess and resulting fuss to keep clean, city fathers claim. City survivors with a scrap of land that will support an apple or plum tree might consider planting.

Even if it's a rental property, the cost is only about $25 per tree. Production takes about 4 years.

A few years back a friend with an orchard rigged a canvas-and-tin funnel-like affair that channeled natural summer and fall breezes through racks of drying plums and peaches. His simple Rube Goldberg device really worked well. He had lots of fruit, and soon he processed literally tons of apples, peaches, and pears. Other than his labor, it was a free-goods enterprise. Word spread, and he started selling all he could produce.

Vegetables such as peppers, zucchinis, red beets, carrots, and corn can also be dried. They all make pretty good food products that keep well up to 5 years. Coming up with sufficient energy to dry can be a challenge, and it takes lots of rehydration water to bring them back before they can be eaten. Like much of this food rehydrated vegetables are bland and monotonous, but they do keep the tummy full.

Proceed exactly the same as with fruits, but drying vegetables usually takes place more rapidly. I personally doubt if survivors will have very many of the above vegetables with exception of carrots and potatoes.

PRESERVING VEGETABLES OUTSIDE

But carrots and potatoes are more easily stored by other methods. In the case of carrots, leave the untreated ones in the ground. Cover them over with a layer of leaves, grass, and duff. In most climates in the continental United States, carrots can be dug and eaten any time till late spring.

Potatoes must have moisture and air moving through them to keep. Some varieties keep much better than others. Red Pontiacs are poor keepers. Spuds with thick, rough-netted skins such as russet Burbanks store quite well. The very best storing potato for survivors is a variety known as Nooksack, named after the Nooksack River in Oregon. They keep like stones. I wish it were otherwise, but this is an obscure variety. It is doubtful that even seasoned gardeners will ever be able to find this variety to grow. But here is how to store all kinds of potatoes:

Dig a fairly large hole in the ground 18 inches deep in a well-drained, somewhat sheltered spot. Line this hole with dry grass and leaves. Place a bushel of spuds in the hole on the lining. Cover with a layer of grass and then 4 inches of soil.

Air and moisture from the soil will move through the potatoes, keeping them in nice condition. Only problem is, once the cache of potatoes is opened, they generally must all be taken and used within the next 30 days. Once disturbed, they all go bad relatively quickly.

Will city survivors have access to tomatoes? In the unlikely event some come your way, store them for the intermediate term as follows. Clip plants at ground level while green tomatoes are still on the vine. Hang these intact vines from the roof in a sheltered, not particularly warm area. Fruit on these vines will slowly ripen, and should be picked from time to time. We have enjoyed fresh, red tomatoes off the vine as late as February after clipping and hanging in October the year previous.

In times past, vegetables were often salted, pickling them in large brine barrels. Results were and still are borderline. But maybe it will be appropriate to try this method again.

At any rate, city survivors should expect to keep very busy putting up the crop at harvest time. Some of this technology is as old as time, but it will all work like a champ in a survival context. The total food supplies we raise or forage from the land and put up one way or another may be modest, but their importance will be tough to overemphasize.

Chapter 8

Emergency Shelter in Cities

Sheltering in built-up areas poses special challenges. Just as in planning for water, food, and energy, three separate and distinct arrangements for shelter must be made. Many city survivors, looking at what other survivors have had to endure in the course of sheltering in big cities, opt for at least four different contingency plans.

Shelter plans in cities are hugely more difficult than in the country. City survivors are always at the mercy of the whims of fate to an extent that astounds country survivors. No one can predict where an errant artillery round might land, where a commander might send his soldiers, or where the tanks may punch through the city. Chances are always virtually 100 percent that one or two contingency shelter plans absolutely will not be workable.

Survivors of Stalingrad, for instance, reported that once fires started in the city, they burned as long as 2 weeks! It was so hot that Soviet soldiers 2 miles away could feel the heat. The sky glowed red for nights on end, and tens of thousands died. German forces did not start the fires and it was well beyond their capacity to put them out, once started.

Dozens of additional considerations must be addressed when picking city shelter locations, in contrast to making similar decisions cut in the country. Hiding and camouflage are the most important elements of a country retreat We could also wish that our country retreat is relatively near our stored supplies and trade goods, water, energy, and some adequate gardening soils. In the city these various components are seldom found together near the retreat.

Hiding is even more important in the city than in the country. So much so that other elements of survival may have to be compromised. In other words, city survivors may find it necessary to walk or ride bicycles a mile or two to secure water, tend their gardens or their livestock. Hiding is so important that frequently other elements of survival are not thought of until lack of food, water, and fuel becomes critical.

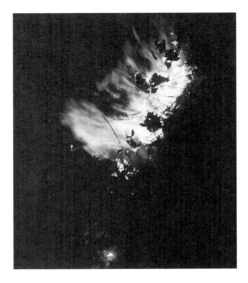

Uncontrolled fires are a danger and scourge in cities.

There are simply too many bad guys, both on our side and on their side, not to hide. It sounds romantic and macho now to claim that you can hold them at bay with superior firepower, but as a practical matter duking it out with any of these people is not practical, especially in the long run.

Family units are the best survival groups. Down through the centuries, family organizations have always survived best, especially in societies with records of strong family ties. At the same time, however, families make terrible combat units. Survivors cannot and will not send sons and daughters out on patrol, suspecting they will likely become casualties.

Another truth learned in the past several hundred years, and in this century in particular, involves the fact that city survivors can-

EMERGENCY SHELTER IN CITIES 121

Never become a refugee. Refugees cannot control their destinies.

Avoid sheltering near government buildings. Major government complexes will be targets of attackers.

not allow themselves to become refugees. Refugees are always subject to the whim and caprice of soldiers, either ours or theirs, and of governments.

The only options for refugees, in either case, are to become dead or become slaves. People already psychologically dependent on government seem to be the ones who elect to become refugees. I cannot understand voluntary refugees in any other context.

City survivors absolutely must hide during the worst of the fighting, leaving the retreat only to move if burned or blasted out or to replenish food, water, and fuel supplies. Survivors may be forced out briefly to tend the garden or the livestock or to dispose of waste. Keep in mind that emergencies have a way of passing, but expect to spend lots of time hunkered down in the retreat.

Being relatively close to water, stored supplies, and tillable ground is helpful, but being far away from certain particularly dangerous places is far more helpful. I have mentioned that my dad lived across the street from a railway switching yard in World War I Germany. Had bombing been carried out to the extent it was in World War II, this could have been a deadly situation.

Good places to avoid today? Government buildings of any kind, armories, supply depots, motor pools, troop billets, refineries, freeway cloverleafs, petroleum storage areas, pipelines, waterworks, telephone exchanges, ammunition factories, power generation and distribution facilities, central freeway interconnection points, major bridges, port facilities, hospitals, apartments where government officials might meet or live, and even places where high government officials go to recreate. As a practical matter, military and survival veterans claim it is almost impossible to know ahead with any certainty which areas of one's city will be targeted during the course of urban conflict. The best we can do is to pick places unlikely to be in the maelstrom. This may provide a perhaps 50-50 chance of being spared, which is certainly not much of a guarantee.

Understanding how aggressor forces might likely sweep into a city might be helpful. Cities overrun and then recaptured over and over again provide some examples, but not much hope. The Warsaw Ghetto comes to mind. Each side expanded its operations till the ghetto was completely trashed. At the end, German SS generals bragged that all buildings in the ghetto were completely pulverized and would now make good construction material.

Two philosophies are always true relative to modern urban warfare. First, attacking soldiers won't move up broad, open thoroughfares into the open arms of defenders. They will move through built-up areas by punching through buildings, especially when these buildings are very large, as in industrial areas, or when they are virtually interlocking, as is true in most European cities and some U.S. cities characterized by row houses.

Second, nondescript, plain vanilla hides well. There are examples of unique retreats, extremely cleverly hidden, but in general, being the 287th house in a basically look-alike suburb provides safety. The same is true of the retreater who is in one of 43 identical apartments in a giant complex.

I was in one of these recently, just north of Washington, D.C. The corridors in these complexes were probably hundreds of yards long. Except for numbers on the doors, everything was shockingly the same. The dreary sameness would have driven me nuts. The fellow I talked with in the complex didn't know the names of either of his next-apartment-over neighbors, but he did know the people across the hall by sight enough to say "hi" when he saw them.

While the drab sameness would have provided some protection, these older apartments seemed to be finished with quite a bit

At times, phony but scary-looking warning signs will discourage soldier and civilian entry. The cost is so low that it's worth trying.

of wood. My first reaction was that fire danger might cancel out any other value hiding in that complex might offer.

City survivors may employ psychological devices that will tend to keep enemy elements at a distance and plant confusion and fear in their minds. Many are extremely effective: these devices give the impression of death and destruction, which should be avoided by intruders at all cost.

The simplest of these involves placing a sign on the door which might read, "custodial storage area," or, "danger, high-voltage power boxes, no unauthorized entry." Another, displaying the universal sign for radiation danger, is a proven winner. In our culture, signs warning of chemical danger or of fumigation danger are extremely effective. At present, signs warning of asbestos also produce great alarm.

In cities it is often easier than that. Rather than official-looking, nicely printed color signs, survivors can easily post hastily made signs warning of chemical danger and poison gas ahead, or that an area is known to contain antipersonnel and antivehicle mines and has not been properly cleared of such. I would even post a warning about snipers working in teams on the area ahead, and that military personnel should understand that the area has not been secured. Warnings of unexploded artillery or mortar rounds or bombs may also be effective.

Will it come to this in the United States? In some cases signs must be written in languages other than English! Warning symbols for chemical or biological weapons or mines, which are universally used without script in any language, may be effective. Will this stuff work? Reports indicate that it often does. I would follow expert recommendation and give these ploys a try.

People, especially in our culture, greatly fear the unknown. Americans are currently irrationally fearful of chemicals and radiation. Soldiers are trained to ignore their fears. But, who knows— you may be lucky and encounter lazy, fearful soldiers.

Other problems may be as pervasive. Slipping in and out for additional supplies of food, water, medicine, and fuel is one that comes to mind. Can rabbits and pigeons be kept close at hand in places convenient to the retreat? Perhaps they can't be kept right in the apartment building, but they can be put in areas accessible to those retreating in the apartment complex.

Like positioning a new McDonald's hamburger joint, three things are vital: location, location, and location. Not only should one's apartment retreat be in a nondescript, nontargeted neighborhood, but it should be in a location where survivors can slip in and out easily. Sometimes this takes creative remodeling! In Beirut, many apartment dwellers punched an additional way out through the wall to a stairwell or to an external fire escape. In one case it was a hole in the ceiling, eventually leading to a hallway out.

We all have heard that the best place to hide a tree is in a forest. For city survivors, this becomes something of a golden rule. There are an incredible number of potential survival shelter locations in built-up areas. Most experienced people say it is relatively easy to find something that will work. When fighting has been especially heavy, driving most citizens out of an area, it is especially easy.

Walk-ups on the fourth floor and above provide great protection so long as the building is not a targeted, defended, or a dominant building in the area. Both attacking and defending forces will frequently attempt to turn a dominant building into a fire or observation center. Don't pick a building likely to become the home of a mortar position or a rocket crew.

High-rise buildings "rubbleized" on the top few floors are excellent retreat locations. Rubble above provides a sort of protective cap. On the street below, chunks of cement, rock, glass, and

EMERGENCY SHELTER IN CITIES

Floors beneath rubbleized portions of buildings can be braced to afford camouflage and protection.

A good supply of plastic tarp and rope is useful to construct temporary shelters.

pieces of jagged steel lying about give an impression of desolation, and may impede some traffic.

Here is a really disgusting suggestion that may provide helpful in some circumstances. When a long-dead, foul-smelling horse, cow, dog, goat, camel, or whatever can be found, pull it into the retreat area. The smell of death may nauseate defenders, but it also deters those with just a curious motive from staying and looking around.

In some cases in Beirut, survivors reinforced top floors of buildings with steel girders and heavy wooden beams. They then intentionally rubbleized the top few floors, both adding protection and giving the impression that the building was vacant and destroyed.

Madrid and Berlin were too early for this technology, but it is amazing how quickly city survivors string up standard blue, green, or brown plastic tarps around the area. Not only are these tarps used to collect drinking water, they close holes in roofs

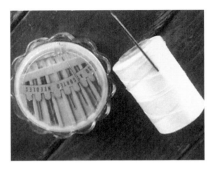 

Needles and thread are essential items which are often overlooked.

City survivors appreciate tents because of their flexibility.

and sides of buildings to keep weather and sun out. They also preclude observation of those inside. After a few days, the presence of one more tarp shelter creates little additional alarm.

Here are some suggestions for those who intend to use plastic tarps as one of their shelter strategies. Don't plan to use overly large tarps, urges our been there, done that crew. These are too difficult to manage and often impossible to obscure, much less hide. A 12-x-20 footer is about right for urban survivors, they claim.

Plan for a large quantity of tough, durable nylon rope, they suggest. No doubt turning these tarps into a kind of improvised shelter is much handier with ample rope. In wild, tough climates, shelters won't survive the first storm unless they are thoroughly anchored.

It is also very important to lay in several large sail needles and ample thread to make emergency repairs. Without means of repair, a torn tarp or one with a hole poked through it or a pulled grommet must be discarded. With needle and thread, repairs are made and life in the shelter goes on, such as it is.

Many city survivors, especially in colder climates, reckon that they could have used small, insulated, highly portable tents. Staying out of harm's way in a city is an incredible challenge. No question that using small two- and three-man tents to move quickly and often would be very helpful. Essentially, they recommend that city survivors camp in various locations in and out of buildings in their city.

Placing an additional tent or two in one's emergency gear is not particularly difficult. But, like knowing about needles and thread

EMERGENCY SHELTER IN CITIES

Many survivors use common, inexpensive fiberglass septic tanks as underground retreats or as containers for potable water.

for repairs, tents are not items city survivors normally think about.

One survivor purchased an old steel 2,000-gallon underground oil tank. It was surplus from an environmentally incorrect service station. It sat for so long in a wrecking yard that the tank no longer smelled of oil. He got it and delivery for $100 cash.

Using a Saws-All, he cut a door in one end of the approximately 5-x12-foot tank. He welded two hinges and a door latch on the steel cutout, providing access and a closing mechanism.

After the tank has been buried into the side of a steep sloping hillside, it is difficult to tell that anything is there. Not only does a buried tank provide emergency shelter, it could also be used to store supplies. The total cost is less than $200, including using a backhoe for installation.

Not everyone can make use of this device, but at least by knowing the idea is out there, city survivors can make up their own minds.

A great many variations—often expensive—on this converted tank-shelter concept have been available. Several city survivors—mostly from the nuclear era—have installed one or two fiberglass septic tanks (linked by 36-inch-diameter pipe) in their backyards, in the floors of their garages, or in the front yard under the rose bushes. These shelters are certainly workable, but are expensive and a bit cramped. Details such as ventilation pipes and access holes must be attended to. Pipes sticking out of the ground can compromise the setup if poorly done.

Some large models of these almost-underground apartments are occasionally advertised in *American Survival Guide*. It's likely that sales of these units are not particularly brisk, which explains why companies offering them seem to come and go rapidly.

It is possible, using cement blocks or even poured concrete, to wall up a corner of a basement, garage, warehouse, or even storage bin, providing a hidden shelter. During the past 20 years I have only seen a few. One was in Indonesia and another in Singapore. The last one was in Tarp, Germany, about 3 miles from the Danish border: this unit extended out under the fellow's garden. The entrance was through a very narrow, cluttered cellar. The owner counted it as one of his life's major accomplishments that he put this shelter in without local authorities approving or even knowing. His ventilation fan was cleverly hidden in a sort of German version of a gazebo.

They don't tell you this in the instruction packet, but to be really successful, any shelters built into lower floors or the basement of existing buildings absolutely must include some sort of device to strengthen the roof above against collapse. Usually these are small steel I-beams or angle iron uprights and cross-members.

Another hideaway I looked at was accessible through an apartment complex and then through a warehouse. Originally this was a very small, now unused manager's office blocked up inside a large warehouse. It seemed to me that this large, unused warehouse could have likely become a storage/repair facility for military vehicles during an emergency, but there was a well-stocked retreat there.

Another suggestion from early literature on the subject is to dig a trench in the ground over which an old vehicle is pulled. This is probably a holdover from the Cold War but it may work again. After moving the vehicle on top of the trench, its wheels are pulled off, marooning it over the chopped-out shelter hole.

Trench retreats probably should be lined with a plastic tarp. At best they have to be misery personified, but a great part of city survival is wanting very badly to survive. Can anyone today imagine living in a wet, dirty place like this? World War I soldiers in the trenches did, but they had a very strong pioneer spirit as well as tremendous will to make the best of it.

Of all these concepts, experts pick camping in old fire- and artillery-damaged or rubbleized buildings as being a second choice after just staying put in one's nondescript, previously prepared retreat. Using tanks, tarps, dugouts, cement-block shelters, and so

EMERGENCY SHELTER IN CITIES

on are all workable. But many of these may not be feasible in your circumstances.

Two additional golden rules of survival round out plans for city survival. I've mentioned the first one before, but it bears repeating: Don't allow others to set your destiny by causing you to become a refugee.

Second, do not get involved in any fighting raging around the retreat. Your contribution will be unmeasurable at best, while risks of drawing people and fire are great. The only exception is when the retreat is hopelessly compromised and it is time to take as many of the bastards along for the ride as possible.

These—and being willing and able to move the retreat at instant notice—are the golden rules of city survival shelters.

Chapter 9

Caching and Storage

As much or more so than any other class of survivor, city survivors should know the difference between caching and storage, as well as how to use these techniques to their advantage.

Storage is the laying in of items that may be essential for life at the retreat. Usually these are items of food and supplies that are not *prima facie* contraband and that, if lost, do not lead to a sudden and catastrophic deterioration of life. Caching is done for items that may be illegal and for which there is no substitute or other source of supply. You could say that storage is hiding and caching is deep hiding.

Of course, this can vary from culture to culture and situation to situation. Guns and ammunition are usually cached, whereas flour, dried peas, and salt are stored. How government officials view these various items determines whether they are cached or stored. Summary execution was the penalty in Nazi Germany for unauthorized possession of a firearm; in the Soviet-occupied Ukraine for unauthorized possession of food; and in medieval England for unauthorized possession of a Bible!

Caching has tactical and perhaps even strategic military significance. Incredibly, caching played a major role in the Battle for Europe, especially in France, Czechoslovakia, Italy, and Yugoslavia.

Caching was also material in Vietnam. It may also eventually be a major factor for freedom in American society. While calling it a conspiracy may be premature, I often wonder why preparedness folks in general, and city survivors specifically, pay so little attention to the vital role of caching.

At the start of World War II in Europe, immediately after the fall of France, British military experts were looking for any help they could get. They searched for some tattered remnants of a group that could act as the nucleus of an insurgency unit. All they could initially discover were a very, very few members of a mostly dispirited Communist Party in France. The Communists were few because their own government had persecuted them before the German occupation and, of course, the Nazis had later ruthlessly hunted them down.

Mostly these Communists were located in Paris, but some were scattered throughout the provinces. Farmers often make ideal partisans, but our records suggest that few, if any, French farmers were Communists at that time.

Initially the British—and eventually the Americans, when they came into the fight—were reluctant to extend aid to Communists of any kind, no matter how worthy the cause. Many European Communists hadn't wanted to fight the Nazis because of Hitler's treaty with Stalin.

During all of 1941, England dropped only nine cache tubes containing weapons and explosives to French Communists. A British expert sent to Paris to gather information alleged two things: First, that French resistance fighters had altogether two ancient rifles and two pistols! All were hopelessly obsolete, and there were only a few rounds of ammo for each. In the case of the pistols, they were still black-powder rounds! Second, such as they were, these weapons were all in caches, the locations of which only a very few cell members knew. Active members at the time were almost all women. Any defections or admissions under torture could potentially collapse the entire movement.

Then it was June 22, 1941, and the German Operation Barbarossa against the Soviet Union was under way. At the same moment, additional war supplies from the United States were finally finding their way into the United Kingdom. In 1942, 201 containers of guns, ammunition, explosives, and medical supplies were air-dropped to the French Resistance. From January 1943 until the liberation of France on August 26, 1944, heaven's gates were opened. Thousands of cache tubes were parachuted into France, Italy, and Czechoslovakia. And it worked. At the end, the French Resistance alone was averaging one German soldier per day!

Was all this risk to bomber pilots flying in with stupid-looking, anonymous silver cache tubes worth it? In some cases we still don't know the real names of the Resistance fighters. We do know that although tens of thousands were caught and killed (3,000 in Lidice, Czechoslovakia, alone in the massacre that was meant to avenge the assassination of SS leader Reinhard Heydrich) that absolutely no German tanks were manufactured in Occupied France, that all rail traffic within France was near impossible, that all major German troop movements were reported to the Allies, and that some experts claim Resistance-induced damage in France was greater than that done by the entire Allied Bomber Command during the same period.

Caching weapons and explosives in densely populated occupied cities, where profitable targets are many, obviously can be—and was—decisive.

Now fast-forward to Vietnam in the 1960s and very early '70s. Here is an entire war cornerstoned on caching. Tons upon countless tons of rifles, ammunition, mines, grenades, machine guns, artillery, mortars, mortar bombs, heavy machine guns, artillery rounds, and even stuff as common as rice, bandages, cooking oil, and shoes, all carried ant-like down the Ho Chi Minh Trail, disappeared underground in South Vietnam.

U.S. GIs reported in dismay that it was completely impossible to keep vehicle inner tubes of any kind around. Viet Cong operatives surreptitiously carried them all off for use as a kind of field-expedient cache tube. Immediately before an engagement, all of them miraculously came out of hiding and into action. Immediately after, all went back underground or under rice paddies again.

U.S. servicemen who have returned to Vietnam during the past few years report that peasants still dredge up left-behind weapon caches in significantly large numbers. This is almost 25 years after disposition. Perhaps there is enough for another revolution, but the Vietnamese seem tired of fighting.

Significantly, at least in my mind, caching was a tactic again successfully deployed by Communists. For the second time in a century, a relatively tiny, insignificant force used the otherwise obscure device of caching critical tools and supplies till the very moment when their deployment would be decisive to win a war.

Storage can also imply hiding and secrecy, but not to the extent of caching. Traditional caches usually contain relatively few supplies. But all these supplies are absolutely critical. These may include a gun or guns, ammunition, silencers, maps, and to some extent optics, radios, and other electronic gear. These last items are much like placing medicine and medical supplies in caches.

Vietnam notwithstanding, caches usually imply long-term storage—sufficiently long that cached electronics gear, glass, and medicines are likely to go out of condition. In France it was often 5 years or more between caching and actual deployment.

Common items in city caches might include a rifle, pistol, ammo, small tent, jacket, flashlight, MREs (having better cache life than other foods), a compass, gloves, and batteries. Some other suggestions might include an aluminum cook kit, rope, magnifying glass. matches, solid-fuel tablets, a pen, paper, and vitamin tablets.

Storage is also for goods over the long term. But storage items generally include goods that are not immediately labeled as contraband, as well as larger quantities of these goods for longer term use. Storage items may also include stocks of trade goods and semiperishables that must be rotated at set intervals. This could include bags of flour or sugar, or 55-gallon barrels of gasoline. But some items, like two-cycle oil, store nicely over the long term and don't need to be rotated.

Let the record note that both storage supplies and cache tubes will always be compromised in our technological society when it becomes politically expedient to do so. In times past, many of us spent a great deal of effort confusing storage and caching. This led to deep-storage techniques involving carefully hidden supplies

Modern rat and mouse poisons are miraculous in their ability to control vermin around shelf-stored food.

Keeping your supplies clean, dry, and safe from pests will be of vital importance.

sealed in plastic garbage cans. This was both a hiding and preservation technique that would have been more easily accomplished by obscurity, caution, and purchasing more suitable storable items.

In that regard, boxes of medical supplies, sealed bags of dried peas, lentils, beans, rice, oil, and salt can more simply be stored on well-built steel or wooden shelves placed in an obscure but dry temperature-controlled portion of an apartment, garage, or basement. About the only real precaution is to keep these goods from rats and mice and from exposure to casual view.

For the first time in recorded history, rats and mice are controllable. Modern, scientifically formulated rat and mouse poisons allow us to store bags of commodities in the open on shelves. Modern rodent poisons are even taste-tested. Rats and mice consume it in preference to anything else, and mortality in the group doesn't produce bait shyness.

As mentioned, purchasing cleaned, treated, sealed bags of commodities rather than raw, farm-run grain, wheat, or dried peas and beans takes care of a great many potential problems. All dirt, chaff, vermin, and whatever have been cleaned from these commodities and, rather than dealing with farmers, this stuff can be purchased at the local grocery.

As much as we don't want to admit it, modern technology makes it possible to find virtually any cache, whenever it is politically expedient to do so. In contrast to World War II and even Vietnam, when modern, super-sensitive underground metal detectors were first coming into use, it is relatively easy to uncover a cache tube today, especially out in the country. That's the bad news. The good news is that it is dramatically easier and less expensive to construct and hide an effective cache.

Sturdy cache tubes can be made using 4- and 8-inch SDR pipe.

Almost all cache tubes are put underground, underwater, or under something. I especially like cache locations under roads. Blacktop and rural gravel roads are especially easy to dig for cache tubes.

During World War II, aluminum cache tubes hidden in salt water were ruined in as little as 4 months: they easily became crinkled, damaged, and leaky, most quickly losing their seal. Currently, cheap, easy-to-use cache tubes can be safely placed just about anywhere. I recently saw one that was kept in a fireplace wrapped in heavy reflective foil and rock wool.

Cache tubes can be made at home using SDR (sanitary drain, refuse) plastic pipe, available in virtually any full-service plumbing

CACHING AND STORAGE 137

shop. In the 4-inch size, there is a heavyweight and lightweight grade. Six- and 8-inch tubing comes only in heavy and extra heavy grades. Because of price and portability, first-time cachers generally try to get by on 4-inch tubes. Eventually, everyone comes 'round to using 8-inch pipe.

An 8-inch cache tube 60 inches long will hold a real load of stuff! Eight-inch tubes hold at least two full-sized rifles, four assault rifles, four or five pistols, and several dozen magazines. These magazines can be loaded two-thirds full, or loose rounds can be dropped in as a kind of packing. Other previously mentioned items such as tents, road tarps, MREs, and flashlights might also go in the tubes, depending on one's circumstances. Some of these tubes get up around 200 pounds each when packed, perhaps arguing for smaller, more portable tubes. Smaller tubes are not generally considered because of their inability to hold some bulky rifles.

As an interesting aside, the French Resistance generally kept larger supplies of ammo and explosives cached separate from guns. Immediately before use, they were all brought together. It is lost in history exactly why. Perhaps it was part of their security plan.

Heavy duty, 4-inch SDR pipe retails for about $.95 per foot. Six-inch pipe costs about $1.55 per foot, and 8-inch—our most commonly used size—is still only about $4.15 per running foot.

End caps must be placed on the tubes. Cache tubes are virtually always buried vertically. This minimizes readings from modern metal detectors that can locate a 3/4-inch steel pipe 35 feet down in the ground!

Once buried vertically, cache tubes are impractical to dig up and use again. Bottom end caps are usually permanently sealed to the pipe with ABS cement. Plain, slip-type end caps for 4-inch pipe cost about $1.50 each. Six-inch caps are $7.00, and common 8-inch slip caps cost a whopping $21.00 each. Top caps are simply slid onto the pipe; no cement is used. In place of ABS cement, use regular automotive grease. Properly done, a positive pressure builds inside the pipe when the cap is slipped on the tube, acting as a deterrent to moisture.

One more precaution before burying. Place a stout disk with a

 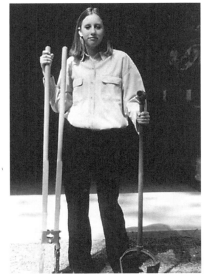

Heavy-duty commercial power augers that dig up to 12-inch holes 7 feet deep with add-on extensions are available from equipment rental shops.

Handtools used to place cache tubes.

sound piece of nylon cord attached to it at the bottom of the tube. This allows the retrieval of small items that may fall to the bottom.

To bury cache tubes, first purchase, borrow, or rent a 10-inch auger-type posthole digger. In times past, 12-inch hand-operated models were available that made this work easier, but these went with the dinosaurs and family farms. But, by slopping the auger around a bit, a 10-inch auger can be made to work with an 8-inch tube. Renting a power unit that bores true 12-inch holes is also possible.

The big problem with either hand or power diggers is getting down a full 6 feet. Cache tubes must be placed no less than 1 foot underground to the top of the pipe.

Lengths of 3/4-inch steel pipe can be used to extend hand-operated auger diggers. Most rental outfits have standard auger extensions they send along, allowing for much deeper holes when using their power augers. Boring one of these holes by hand is

CACHING AND STORAGE

labor intensive and time consuming. At best, plan for one or two cache tube holes per afternoon.

Try to be clever about tube placement. For starters, never hide tubes in the septic system or sewer. It's the first place federal agents look! Inside cities attempt to place cache tubes as far from the retreat as practically possible. Every doubling of distance creates four times as much territory to examine. That's enough that if you haven't bragged about the cache's existence: authorities may be discouraged and give up on the project.

Cities are also full of cables, wires, buried junk, pipes, and other metal clutter. Near these obstructions are wonderful places to bury caches in contrast to the country, expert metal detector users claim.

But leaving cache tubes to revisit storage methods and philosophies, I am often asked how one can go about implementing a foolproof storage plan that won't leave big holes in one's storage inventory after it is too late to add more items. There is a plan that is something of a Golden Rule of Storage Accumulation, but it only works when there are at least 14 months remaining to crisis time. Survivors in Kosovo, for instance, could no longer make any use of this plan.

Start by working your way through your own basic Rule of Threes. For instance, what supplies are required to implement your own development of three energy, food, shelter, and water requirements? Carefully calculate all the tools and implements needed that can either be scrounged after commencement of the crisis or, more realistically, should be on hand before it hits.

In the instance of water, this might include five or six covered plastic buckets to carry water, five or six plastic tarps to collect water, a large supply of nylon rope with which to deploy the tarps, a wooden carrying rack for the buckets, plastic barrels, pipe, bleach, chemicals to make bleach, filter racks, sand, handpumps, well pipe, and whatever other specific items might be required to run a three-element water enterprise.

Do the same for food. Specific recommendations were covered in the food chapter. No need to list these again.

But what about livestock-keeping supplies, including cages, feed, water dishes, and sources of breeding stock? Some of these should be stockpiled now. What about guns and ammo to collect wild and semiwild game? Will traps and snares be required? Better plan for these as well.

Energy requirements are similar. Many of us rely on a pipe to bring natural gas into our homes, or on oil, firewood, or even heat pumps. Will there be generators to power freezers and some minimal heat and light? Should large LP gas tanks or diesel fuel tanks be purchased, buried, and filled? Some city survivors have as many as twelve or fifteen 55-gallon barrels of diesel fuel or gasoline tucked away in mini-storage units listed under an assumed name. Burning scrap wood is a fine plan for city survivors, but what about a stove or simple device in which to burn this wood? Are there sufficient matches to last a year or more?

Are portable tents and sleeping bags one element of your shelter plan? Several tents in good repair, as well as eight or 10 plastic or canvas tarps should be placed in

The idea is not to turn your storage area into a survival supermarket, but rather to store items you know will be necessary, based on past experience.

Common nails are often overlooked as survival goods. They are also valuable trade items.

CACHING AND STORAGE

storage. Rope, it was mentioned, is always in short supply. Currently it is easy to stock up on it—just go to the hardware store and buy what is needed, all to be placed in storage.

Often city survival sheltering is more a matter of preparing for several different possible city collapse situations, and of being sufficiently flexible to camp here and there. This is more important than making a great, long list of needed supplies. After tents, tarps, rope, and a few tools, that's about it.

All this notwithstanding, there really is a Golden Rule of Survival Storage that infallibly leads to each survivor having pretty much all of the stuff he or she needs for his or her own use and for trade. As mentioned, this plan works wonderfully, but not overnight. This plan involves double-buying all goods, commodities, and supplies in the current scheme of one's normal shopping. Absolutely every time a purchase is made, that purchase should be evaluated for survival storage and trade potential. When it fits, buy two or more.

In real life it worked like this, just last week, for me. Our shopping list included the following:

- A 2-gallon yard and garden pressure-type hand sprayer. I bought one extra to trade.
- Fifty pounds of wheat flour. A 50-pound bag of flour lasts us 7 months. We already had one extra, but I decided to purchase two more.
- Light bulbs. Always a valuable commodity. I bought a whole shopping cart full, mostly to go into trade goods.
- Freezer wrap paper. I bought two extra rolls as well as five extra rolls of tape.
- Sugar. We are pretty well stocked ahead, but it's currently very inexpensive, so an extra 25 pounds went in the trade goods.
- Frozen pizza. Probably would be valuable trade goods, but after thinking a bit, I decided I didn't want to fool with it. Nothing extra purchased.
- Box of wire—one for me and one for storage.
- Ballpoint pens. Always a use for these. One dozen to the office, one dozen to the shelf.
- Tomato and cream of mushroom soup. I bought a case of each

to rotate the older cases out of storage and into the pantry for current use. Some of these have been on the shelf for almost 6 years now.
- Gallon can of olive oil. We didn't have this in storage. One gallon for use and one for the shelf.
- Canned capers—we enjoy these a lot but in an emergency we can do without. Nothing more purchased.
- Fifty pounds of 16-penny nails. Disaster averted, as I just used the last of my previous supply. Now we are back up to 50 pounds again plus 50 on the storage shelf that are only touched in an emergency. This reminded me to check other nails and screws. I also bought a gross box of 2-inch #8 wood screws and 50 pounds of 6-penny nails.
- Toilet paper. I don't know how much of this we have in storage, surely quite a lot. This is always an item that will be in demand. I bought three additional 24-roll packages.

There were several other items that I considered, but they have already been forgotten. Not even the brightest man in the world could list everything without leaving holes. But, no doubt, readers get the idea.

Paying for all these goods is always a limiting factor. That's why purchasing a little at a time each week has so much charm. Perhaps looking at all this as an investment that will eventually pay great dividends will help. Also, expenses cycle a bit. After being in the program for a time, weeks will go by when nothing extra is purchased.

Other months there will be expensive batteries, fuel, gloves, jackets, flashlights, buckets of soap, tarps, rope, and a million other items.

It all depends on your level of commitment and dedication, and your personal will to survive.

Chapter 10

Trading

Trading is a significant component of city survival. The past 100 years' experience demonstrates that those who understand and prepare for the process do well. Others don't.

Our understanding of how we might use trading to survive in the city has changed dramatically. Survivors must be extremely practical people. They absolutely must engage in activities that work, even if it means breaking moral or religious codes. A Moslem who wants to survive, for example, would have to ignore his religion's taboos about pork if that were the only food around. How do we know what actually works? Again, by looking around us at actual city survival situations.

Some of the devices to follow will upset some city survivors. This is because these devices do not fit into their preconceived notion of how they fervently wish events would unfold. Let the record note that I wish that our government would collapse and that we could start anew with one based on freedom rather than legal plunder. But looking out over the various countries in the world, there is little cause for hope. We just don't see this happening.

Electing to vigorously pursue some trading strategies will be tough because we really don't want them to work. The use of U.S. dollars as a medium of exchange is an excellent example.

Paper currency marked from one million to 20 million German marks, flanked by a U.S. $100 bill, which is currently the world standard. Worthless Cuban and Zairean currency notes are seen on the right.

MONEY

Only a government can take perfectly good paper, cover it with perfectly good ink, and create perfectly worthless money. There's no argument that our money has been mercilessly debased and devalued over the past few decades.

It has already been established that those with their financial houses in good order will have the best chance of surviving. Great numbers of examples out of history prove this point. Cubans with money for boats and fuel were able to make it to Mexico, the United States, and Spain early on. Chinese with money are currently emigrating to Canada. Rhodesians with cash are now sprinkled all around the world. They didn't all make it, but only Jews with lots of cash had a chance of getting out of Nazi Europe. Later they had the only real chance of getting to Palestine, before it became Israel. I have even encountered an extremely wealthy, former high-

TRADING

At this outdoor market in Cuba prices are publicly posted in Cuban pesos, but privately everything is transformed into dollars.

ranking Nazi living in the United States who used his considerable money to buy connections that eventually got him and much of his loot out of post-World War II Europe.

As much as I hate to admit it, the medium of exchange for the foreseeable future appears to be U.S. dollars. This, I realize, is something of a reversal of my past position. But if the late 20th century has taught us anything, it is that politicians hold on and on. Mexicans, Russians, Poles, South Africans, Kenyans, and just about everybody collects dollars. Not euros, not Swiss francs, not German marks, not Hong Kong dollars, and certainly not Chinese renminbi or Japanese yen. The yen was once considered one of the strongest currencies, but 8 years of grinding recession finally wore it down.

I will gladly change my position on U.S. dollars when I see something coming that will also grind them down. Then I can trade my dollars for hard goods and consumables that always have value.

In times past, U.S. dollars, British pounds, German marks, and Swiss francs were equally prized by traders throughout the world. No longer. Everything is U.S. dollars—even in agricultural villages in remote Mexico, prices are quoted in dollars.

It's kind of like being the chief leper in a leper colony. Because national finances are run so very poorly in most other countries, our own post-freedom economy stands out as being strongest.

New Zealand may be the only exception! Although New Zealand is headed in the correct direction economically and politically with increased emphasis on freedom it currently is experiencing a severe recession. This isn't of their own doing. Traditionally New Zealand exported raw materials to Asia while importing many manufactured goods. The collapse of Asian markets and 2 years of El Niño-induced agricultural failure has taken its toll.

At any rate, New Zealand's economy is and always will be too small to be much of a player in world markets. This also may be what happened to little Switzerland—it is a good economy but it's too small to be influential.

America's economy is so very large that it will dominate for the foreseeable future. Here is another example. While living in rural Africa, I frequently came across original Maria Theresa thalers being used in trade. This was 70 years after the collapse of the Austro-Hungarian Empire. Certainly things move much faster these days, but even if the United States does somehow manage to collapse, it may still take years before people realize that its dollars are worthless.

At this writing absolutely everything worldwide is denominated in U.S. dollars. Oil, refinery products, computers, wheat, corn, gold, precious and nonprecious metals, iron, steel, cocoa, lumber, cases of tomatoes, melons, tobacco, and even a night with a woman. I can't think of anything not denominated and traded worldwide in dollars. As a practical matter, if there were no U.S. dollars we would have to invent them!

Dollars are even being sent rather than food to refugees in ravaged, war-torn areas. It's the trendy new way of arranging for food aid. Dollars in refugees' hands, we have found, encourage the inflow of food by private shippers and producers from hundreds of miles away. As prices go up, local farmers are encouraged to plant more. Aid organizations sending food shipments into an area discourage farmers by lowering prices in their markets. When it's done by government agents, it is always handled in a corrupt and inefficient manner. Money gets the economy running again, whereas actual bags of foodstuffs depress it.

The bottom line—especially for city survivors who will be close to quantities of goods and services—is that storing lots of cash has the potential to overcome great deficiencies in one's survival plan. However, gold—including gold coins—is a poor trade good.

Cuba's economy has been in a state of collapse since the demise of the Soviet Union in 1991 when all Soviet aid to Cuba was halted. I have been there twice since that time. Under-the-counter barter in the tightly knit Cuban society keeps its economy afloat, but this is barter of my two chickens for your cabbage and dozen eggs, or my skill and labor to repair your Soviet-built motorcycle in exchange for your sugar ration. While there I traded extensively in the underground economy using dollars, but never for gold coins. They wouldn't have known what to do with gold: gold of any kind had absolutely no practical value to Cubans. It was much the same in East Berlin before the wall came down. Mexicans are in the same boat. Their economy has been devastated by recent massive peso devaluations and they want gringo dollars, not gold coins.

Gold coins are somewhat similar to the piano my dad's family traded for three sacks of potatoes. Apparently the only reason this deal was finally consummated was out of some sort of perverse sense of humor on the owner's part. Like the piano, gold packs too much value into too little space for owners ever to realize its full potential. It won't do to trade the piano one piece at a time.

Gold coin does meet the survivor's Rule of Portability, but other trade goods do this job better. On the other end of the trade spectrum, small gold coins are also difficult to handle. Teensy, tiny $1 and $5 gold pieces might even blow away in the wind! Our current experience indicates that gold is not a good exchange medium in a primitive survival economy.

TRADE GOODS

Portability, practicality, and profitability are the three P's of trade goods. Profitability has to do with things that are used as tools to create wealth. In most cases, wealth for city survivors is food, water, and shelter. What items should be stocked as trade goods? They have to be consumables!

This fact was reinforced again with visits to Cuba and Britain. Cuban cigar rollers still work on a piece basis. In very un-communist fashion, they are paid by performance the same as any other entrepreneur. Experienced cigar rollers are the best-paid laborers on the island. What did these top-of-the-line laborers want to trade from me? Not gold coins, not CD/tape players, not my watch, or anything else so exotic. It was common, dull, average things like bars of soap and aspirin tablets.

This is similar to what happens to me in Britain. On hearing my American accent, Brits around often position themselves so it is possible to quietly ask if I have any pistol ammunition I wish to trade!

Consumables

Consumable items such as ammunition, soap, film, medicine, toothpaste, toilet paper, shoes, underwear, aspirin, pens, pencils, paper (I was continually asked for these last simple little items in Cuba), cooking oil, salt, wire, wire snares, computer disks, nitrogen fertilizer, blasting caps, gloves, tape, knives, sharpening stones, matches, saws, files, chain saw parts, light bulbs, garden hose, motor oil, engine filters, powder, primers, bullets, canning lids, plastic freezer bags, electrical supplies, nylon rope, coffee, welding rod, batteries, lamp mantles, LP gas, flour, yeast, detergent, needles and thread, tape, bleach, toothbrushes, antacid, sugar, steel wool, calcium hypochlorite (used to home-manufacture bleach), nails, screws, bolts, flashlights, batteries, bulbs and repair parts, tires, pepper, boot oil, and shoelaces all have potential as city survival trade goods.

It's very sobering to contemplate, but apparently the higher the casualty rates among fellow residents, the more these items will be scrounged up and put on the market. There were, for instance, so many German casualties at Stalingrad that hordes of Soviet soldiers enjoyed adequate supplies of captured boots and coats when the shooting died down—some for the first time since they had been in the army.

The importance of simple flashlights in a collapsed city economy is easily overlooked. There are never enough of these. Flashlights and batteries were the principal items we used in our little company store to manipulate the economy of some rural African communities in which I worked. In a few cases we charged up to a full day's wages for a new set of flashlight batteries. The principle employed here may be identical to those we will likely encounter in city survival situations. Africans in the area were happy to work, but could see no reason to work. There were no stores in which they could spend wage money. By opening a company store and carefully orchestrating prices and availability of

Consumables make excellent trade items in collapsed economies.

some especially desirable items, we were able to both get our work accomplished and provide a benefit to our workers.

In many regards it was similar to our own society. (Except here it's the politicians' running the government store that forcibly takes away our money in the form of taxes to finance showy, makework projects.) Placing money on a cord to wear around their necks as a means of ornamentation was common among rural Africans. This was of little economic benefit to the Africans. Providing flashlights, bulbs, and batteries they desperately needed was a benefit. It was never mandatory that they buy from us. When other stores opened we closed ours. Money is money and is always fungible.

Obviously the above list is at least 5,000 items fewer than complete. All of these items share the characteristic of being small, portable, somewhat durable, and almost essential in many circumstances. They are also all consumables. The only variation is that some of the desirable items are capital goods or tools—as things with which to make other things are called.

These are my favorite trade goods. Based on past experience, especially in large cities, I like ammunition, matches, and flashlights and batteries. Thirty years ago, for example, I purchased 1 million rounds of ammunition from Interarmco in Alexandria, Virginia. The cost was 2 cents per round. On the way home I was really concerned. What were we going to do with all this 8mm Lebel, 8 x 57mm and 7 x 57mm Mauser, .303 British, and other assorted pistol ammo? Not to worry, the boss advised. Unlike firearms, which are not generally consumed, ammunition is used up in large quantities. Guns that use this stuff will probably still be here in 50 years, but ammunition supplies are always shrinking. He was right. We put a price of 8 to 10 cents per round on the ammo. In 6 weeks enough was sold to pay for the entire original purchase. The last 80 percent was profit.

Wholesale ammunition dealers currently report sales of tens of millions of rounds of ammunition. Every time the government beats the gun control drum, citizens start laying in even more ammunition. Eventually all of this will come out again in one form or another. Perhaps I am wrong and there will be no scarcity. But scarcities are often regional. I wouldn't take chances on not having enough ammo on the outside chance that there will be too much to trade when cities go down. If you as a city survivor do not have enough ammo of the correct kind, it will be very serious indeed.

Lowly, cheap kitchen matches are another often overlooked trade item that is always in tremendous demand by city survivors. Several characteristics of matches quickly lead to this circumstance. Unless we smoke, under normal circumstances of life we currently use relatively few matches. As a result, nobody thinks about them. In survival circumstances, especially in cities, we will have opportunity to use scores of matches every day. We will need matches for lighting stoves, lamps, cookers, smokers; starting fires; burning trash; and dozens of other uses that will quickly become apparent.

Difficult as it is to believe, city survivors report using about three 250-match boxes per month! Careful conservation can cut this to about two boxes per month. But I would prefer to purchase and store a bale of matches now while they are easily available.

Some types of trade goods are frequently viewed with a jaundiced eye even by city survivors in desperate circumstances. Home-canned meat and vegetables are good examples. People just will not trade for something unknown that they think might have potential to harm them. Convincing them that you eat this same stuff every night might work, but don't be surprised when it doesn't!

Reloaded ammunition is another of these suspicious items. Amateur gun owners are fearful of reloads, while experienced gun owners already reload their own ammunition. Little demand remains in the middle for reloads. Test this theory at your next gun show. Take a big box of reloaded ammo in and see what kind of offers you get. Desperation could turn this philosophy a bit; we will have to see. In the interim, don't get too excited when reloads are not viewed as desirable trade goods.

Medicine

Fresh medications in original sealed bottles stamped with current expiration dates are always very desirable. Out-of-date or scruffy-looking medications are viewed with suspicion. Individuals without needed medications are often forced to pay virtually any price to secure vital supplies. I recently encountered a dramatic example in Cuba. A mid-ranking bureaucrat working in the government tourist bureau had a seriously epileptic 4-year-old daughter. We believed that her ever-more-frequent seizures would soon lead to permanent damage. Absolutely none of the medication the little girl desperately needed was available in Cuba. Her father was willing to pay any price for drugs that would only have cost $8 at most in American pharmacies.

The point, of course, is that some drugs in some specific circumstances will be priceless. Everything we currently use should be stockpiled in a goodly quantity. Most drugs gradually lose their vitality when kept past their expiration date. Freezing helps prolong the life of many medicines, arguing again for use of a freezer in city survival circumstances.

Accumulating medical supplies for possible sale or trade is, at best, an extremely complex, elusive issue. It is compounded by the fact that our society does not trust its citizens with drug purchase decisions. Not only do we not know which medications might be in demand, we have trouble getting them within our current system.

Nevertheless, in spite of great resistance from the ruling elite medical profession, drugs can be accumulated for trade. Summarizing very briefly, these sources can be the following:

1. Sympathetic medical professionals who surreptitiously supply needed medications to be stockpiled by survivors.
2. The local livestock health counter, which offers veterinary medical supplies. These drugs, intended for animals, are safe, clean, and effective.
3. Counterfeit prescriptions—those authorizing pieces of paper—

which are easy to make on a home computer. Stay away from any narcotics to avoid attention.
4. Importation from foreign countries where laws are not so monopolistic. Do this either in person or by mail. Pioneered in the late 1980s by AIDS patients, this has become a major source of supply for many people.
5. Cross-use of more easily obtained, over-the-counter medical supplies. Potent hemorrhoid medication, for instance, containing high percentages of Lidocaine can be used as topical pain killers when sewing up wounds.

I have written two books on this complex subject. Those with a sense of understanding and interest in medical procedures and medications will do well to secure copies of *Survivor's Medicine Chest* and *Do-It-Yourself Medicine*. Both are available from Paladin Press, and the information in them is not repeated here.

Luxuries

The durability of luxury goods as trade items always amazes and shocks me. There is something about consumption of this class of goods that touches a nerve, especially when trading with people in life-and-death circumstances. Often we see obviously poor people living on the brink of survival trading for expensive shoes, watches, makeup, jewelry, booze, and tobacco. There may be some hidden linkage, but it is often difficult to see how ownership of these goods adds to one's chances for survival.

Often we see luxury goods traded for long-term durable goods such as a set of wrenches, a shovel, or my all-time favorite, ax or maul handles (which are completely, absolutely irreplaceable in any real survival circumstance). My old granddad wouldn't even own a car. "Can't make money with a car," he claimed, so he always owned and drove a truck. Cars can be used in business as well as trucks, but granddad had a point. The same philosophy seems to hold true for luxury goods. How one will create a better survival situation for himself and those at the retreat with a box of cigars rather than a shovel is now beyond the scope of this book. So we

Trading services for goods isn't usually wise for the holders of goods, unless the service is of unusual value.

drop the question. Preparing to profit from such human failing is also a question. Do we really lay in cases and cases of fine whiskey in the hope and belief we will be able to trade for vital goods? I suspect not.

Labor

Trading skilled labor for consumables or capital goods is frequently done in city survival situations. An electrician trading his skill to rebuild a generator for an extra tire for his trailer comes to mind as an example. Time is very much of a premium in all true survival situations, so this isn't quite a matter of trading nothing for something. But almost.

People rapidly become experts at something in absolutely every survival situation. Even American Indians specialized. Survivors in Beirut, Berlin, Madrid, or wherever we look all specialized. It's the nature and core of survival as those in the remaining society re-establish some sort of economic order. The reason survivors are so busy is because they often perform tasks they are not good at, using tools not specifically designed for the task.

The rule in cases where a survivor must engage outside specialized help is, as much as possible, to offer to trade their skilled labor for your skilled labor rather than giving up scarce ammunition-batteries-matches-type trade goods. This won't work in the case of a need for a brain surgeon, but you certainly understand the concept.

BARGAINING

Bargaining in survival situations, either for money or for other goods, will be common. Most Americans have no clue how to bargain. Some consider the exercise to be tacky.

Here is a brief summary of a nonthreatening method of bargaining that is usually effective and does not impinge on the desire of most Americans not to be confrontational. Americans really don't like to come right out and tell the other guy his stuff is priced too high and that they will only offer so much. This is too rude and abrupt, even for city survivors who, in prior lives, may have been very rude and abrupt.

Begin by determining that the other guy really has something you need at the retreat. In survival situations, it is common for owners not to display valuable goods till the deal is fairly far along. If you have nothing he particularly wants, then assume the deal will have to be for cash. This original posture should be stretched out as long as possible. Part of any successful bargaining technique involves inducing the other party to invest time in the process.

Perhaps it is time spent listening to information about the quality of the item. Maybe it's the item's history or the owner's history, his current survival problems, health of his wife and kids, the grandkids, weather, sources of supply, position of the enemy or whatever. Americans tend not to be listeners. But in this case you gotta spend at least 15 minutes earnestly BS-ing and listening.

When he finally gets around to setting his price, don't react by saying it's too high. Simply tell him that this item is exactly what you need and want, that it is in the condition you hoped for, and that he has talked you into the item. You like the item so much you only wish you could afford it. Lay it on thick about wanting the item, but it is out of your reach financially. At times sellers will voluntarily lower their price, without a buyer's counteroffer.

Make up some lame excuse why you can't afford the item. "Just traded my last two flashlights for a generator belt," says you. Also, be mentally prepared to simply walk away from the deal if the seller doesn't respond.

Usually the seller will ask how much you can afford to pay.

Don't lowball him, which will expose the game. Simply say he could help out a bunch by selling it for X amount. At this point, it is incumbent upon you to find some reason for the fellow to help by lowering his price. Usually this reason originates in the initial conversation. Maybe it's the offer of your help in your special area of expertise in the future.

The main goal is not to confront him harshly or be belligerent in any way, but to keep on talking in a manner that convinces the seller that he should help you and that it is now his problem to make the sale.

By not being confrontational when no deal is made, it is easily possible to come back the next day with another offer. You might claim, "I found another 5 gallons of gas in our storage area," or whatever.

This is exactly the system used throughout the Orient, where saving face is of utmost importance. It also nicely fits most Americans' personalities. After practice, count on at least a 75-percent success ratio.

Chances to trade for necessary and even unnecessary items are far greater in the city than they are in the country. More people and more goods lying about to trade for make this possible. Some survivors, who by luck or chance happen to store the correct trade goods, can make up for complete ignorance or lack of planning. Some will make a fortune. I wouldn't want to play it this close, but the been there, done that crew claims it frequently happens.

Chapter 11

Guns

Ownership and deployment of proper firearms is a sufficiently serious consideration for city survivors that an entire chapter on the subject seems appropriate.

While I believe good evidence exists to support my belief that country survivors could get by without firearms, other experience screams that city survivors absolutely must have adequate guns of the correct type. The idea that country survivors could get by without guns is based on the real-life experience of Bill Moreland, who lived alone without contact with any other humans for 13 years. Moreland's adventure is relatively recent. He survived in Idaho's rugged Clearwater National Forest from 1932 to 1945. Incredibly, Moreland had a .22-caliber rifle with perhaps 25 rounds of ammunition for only the last 2 years of his saga.

Personal experiences of city survivors during the past 30 years abundantly demonstrate that all city survivors will have far too many opportunities to defend their area. They will also seriously (perhaps fatally) cripple their survival food plans by not being able to shoot the occasional dog, cat, rat, goat, or duck if no guns are available. The experiences have convinced me that city survival is impossible without adequate firearms and the knowledge of how to use them.

Some of the guns and ammunition mentioned below are tough to acquire. Rather than belaboring this issue, I assume that successful survivors will be people of tenacity, perseverance, and resourcefulness. A silencer is a good example of something that will test a survivor's resolve. Under most city survival circumstances in the United States they are very illegal. At the same time, silencers—or something like them—are essential.

Many survivalists like myself have discovered perfectly workable substitutes for silenced weapons. These are inexpensive, relatively easy to make, and legal. Some readers will demand the real thing. Since many, many books are out there on the subject of homemade silencers, I won't try to cover that information here.

The first serious problem I encountered while researching this chapter involves the fact that even average Americans who know little about guns know infinitely more about them than survivors of Beirut or Berlin who may have actually shot it out with marauding intruders.

Here is an example. City survivors will definitely need sniper rifles, I was told with great seriousness and enthusiasm by an Arab friend from Beirut.

"So what constitutes a sniper rifle?" I asked.

"It's one with a telescopic sight," I was informed. To me, a sniper rifle is a tactical rifle capable of 4-inch groups at a minimum 800 yards. This fellow was actually describing what we commonly refer to as a deer rifle.

Are accurate 500-yard shots inside cities sufficient? Perhaps yes and perhaps no. Firearms are always very personal matters. My position is that sniper rifles of some sort are extremely important, and that an 800- to 1,000-yard rifle will also do well at 500 yards. But it doesn't work the other way around.

My analysis of this Beiruti fellow's grasp of this subject was complicated by the fact that, although he had been an active soldier engaged in fighting in the city, he had no clue regarding differences between hunting and sniper rifles. He did not even know how to sight in a rifle with optic sights!

Israeli army tacticians started it with development of their Uzi submachine guns. Instead of taking careful aim, the concept here was

Sniper rifles will ground these machines just as effectively as a 20mm cannon.

to let a hail of bullets fly in the direction of a potential target, who cowered to hide or ran in terror.

The concept of just firing toward a target rather than taking aim became doctrine in the Middle East and then in the old Soviet army. Things are slowly changing back again, but we still see military units today composed of infantry who engage the enemy by firing AK-47s blindly around corners or over the tops of barriers. There are also increasing numbers of soldiers who carry what we might refer to as scope-sighted deer rifles. They are called snipers, but these are the guys who are supposed to shoot at specific enemy targets out to the limit of their weapon's range (about 500 to 600 yards). Will shooters aiming at an enemy again outnumber general-direction shooters? Changes seem to be occurring. How far they go is anybody's guess.

My personal conviction is that true long-range, superaccurate sniper rifles are the next wave. This is principally because these weapons can inflict incredible material damage on enemy equipment without actually physically engaging enemy personnel. For those who can really acclimate themselves to coldly shooting another human, sniper rifles can also be a real deterrent to invaders. Shoot the pilot or ruin his helicopter on the ground; the results are similar.

There is always the danger of fighting this war with last war's technology. Sniper rifles may fall into that category, but for the foreseeable future they seem to have secured their role as destroyers of valuable, often irreplaceable property from great distance and as a deterrent to infantry. It also seems that after a veritable explosion of recent sniper rifle technology, things have stabilized to some extent. It's a good time to put a sniper rifle together.

A Sako L691 action is an excellent basis for sniper rifle.

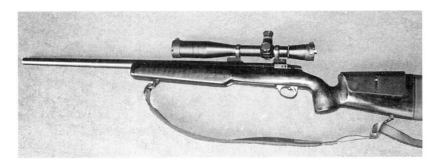

Accurate ultra-long-range sniper rifles are costly and time consuming to assemble, but for city survivors, their ability to destroy valuable equipment at long range is priceless.

ASSEMBLING A SNIPER RIFLE

Assembling a tactical rifle takes at least 18 months and about $2,000. City survivors who might need this type of equipment are well advised to get cracking. Not only does assembling all the components take time, it only takes one nut to bring the wrath of the government down on these weapons. Absolutely everyone with any qualifications who makes these weapons is currently booked ahead about 6 to 8 months. If new regulations are proposed, prices will zoom skyward and waiting lines will become hopeless.

There are, of course, many ways to proceed. First and easiest, but not usually best, is to purchase a completely assembled, heavy-barreled Winchester or Remington sniper rifle. Because these stock packages are not usually 1/4-minute-of-angle grade without further tuning

GUNS

Properly mounting a scope can be expensive and complicated. Fortunately, this is the last step to putting together a genuine tactical rifle.

by a competent sniper rifle gunsmith, this is not usually considered to be the best course of action.

Bill Hicks and Co., Ltd., 15155 23rd Avenue North, Minneapolis, MN 55447, often seems to have the best inventory of these types of rifles. Hicks is a wholesaler, so one would have to ask a local dealer to order for them.

Most basic actions used in tactical rifles require extensive hand turning on the part of skilled gunsmiths who have worked on many rifles of this type. One dramatic exception includes rifles and actions manufactured by Sako in Finland. Sakos are usually very accurate right out of the box. Alas, bare Sako actions are not imported in large numbers. When one is found for sale, the price will be high to very high. Bill Hicks and Co., Ltd., is often a good place to inquire about Sako actions. If not, contact Stoeger Industries, 5 Mandsard Court, Wayne, NJ 07470, to find out which wholesale distributors recently took delivery on a number of actions. Probably it will be a Sako Model L691 Mag action unless you intend to try and make a much smaller .308 or .223 into a tactical rifle. Sako's small actions are Model S49s.

The price when an action is finally located will be about $375. That's what the last one cost me.

Several excellent gunsmiths in the United States have experience making tactical rifle barrels and fitting them to actions. No matter who does this work, be double sure to ask how many tactical rifles he has done in the past. Experience at this business is not only handy, it is vital.

Brian Sipe, of the Montana Rifleman, 1765 Montana Highway #35, Kalispel, MT 59901, has done most of the tactical rifle barrels on guns I have put together. However, Sipe is often booked solid 7 to 10 months ahead. Mel Doyles, RR 2, Box 196M, St. Maries, ID 83861, is another good hand at this business.

Most of the tactical rifles I have assembled have been in .300 Winchester Magnum. Equipped with 26-inch barrels, they shoot out about 3,200 feet per second using 168-grain Hornaday boattail National Match bullets. Off-the-shelf ammo is not available. Start with 68 grains of 4831 powder in handloads.

Tactical rifles have been built in .308, .30-06, and even .223, but these cartridges present too many additional trajectory problems, especially for initially unpracticed users. On the other end of the spectrum, we are currently working on a .30/.378 tactical rifle. It is made to use .378 Weatherby Magnum cases necked to .30 caliber. This may be overkill rather than underkill, as is true with the smaller family of cartridges.

The cost to barrel and cut a chamber is about $400, depending on whether it is fluted, has a removable muzzle brake, or deviates from the standard 1:10 twist. Our fluted, barreled rifles have not shot better than plain barrels, even when shot very hot, which should never happen in real life with tactical rifles. Even if the rounds are delivered over a matter of hours, the maximum rounds from one position—even in a combat situation—is always three! After that your position will be dangerously exposed.

Longer, heavier 26-inch barrels, measuring .90 inches at the muzzle tapered back to 1.25 inches at the breech, with a tactical rifle recessed crown cut in them, are very important to the success of the project. These larger, heavier barreled action sets absorb heat and recoil to great advantage.

The next task is bluing. Mel Doyles usually does this work for me. His dull-black ranch finish is especially practical for tactical rifles. These finishes don't glare or shine. The cost for a polished "in the white" action and barrel is about $50.

Securing a proper military/tactical stock correctly fitted to a

Sako barreled action is not particularly quick, easy, cheap, or convenient. Figure on another 6 to 10 months' wait. Off-the-shelf stocks either fit poorly, are too difficult to finish-fit, are too wimpy, or lack necessary features characteristic of genuine tactical stocks.

Only two places I know of currently manufacture and fit genuine military-style/grade stocks to Sako barreled actions. Both claim to supply the U.S. Army and the Marines, but be prepared for sticker shock. Both are named McMillan and are both are located in Phoenix, Arizona. (Probably the result of a family disagreement or something.)

But not to worry. They both do excellent work, in my experience. Prices are so similar they may someday face anti-trust action from the government.

McMillan Fiberglass Stocks, Inc., 21421 N. 14th Avenue, Suite B, Phoenix, AZ 85027 and McMillan Gunworks, Inc., 302 W. Melinda Lane, Phoenix, AZ 85027, both have extremely nice, full-color brochures listing their various styles of stocks and options available with each model. In my opinion, builders are not in the ballpark unless they order an adjustable buttplate, cheekpiece, and custom laser bedding. This will cost around $500.

It is by now close to 2 years since we embarked on this project. Expenses are up around $950 to $1,300, depending on options, and not including dozens of long-distance calls. Purchasing a suitable scope and mount is the next and last big hit. Mounting the scope has traditionally been tougher and more expensive than it should be. On my last tactical rifle completed 3 or 4 months ago, I had to go back and spend an extra $250 for more suitable, workable mounts. Even after acquiring great amounts of experience, opportunities to do it wrong are still great.

Part of the difficulty involves the fact that true tactical scopes are virtually always made up on 30mm tubes. Differences in field of vision, clarity, and utility between 25mm hunting scopes (1 inch) and 30mm ones are dramatic. Very few people understand the nuances of a 30mm tube versus a 25mm tube until they start to practice with them.

Mounting a nontactical hunting-type scope on a first-class sniper rifle is almost always an error. Hunting scopes are not sufficiently rugged and they lack easy rear read-and-adjust dials that make use of previously prepared "come-up" or trajectory cards possible. These cards are used to preprogram the rifle to shoot accurately from 350 to 1,000 yards by simply setting the dials to predetermined readings. My choice of scope is the same one used by the U.S. Marines, many police SWAT teams, and Navy SEAL teams. It is a 16-power Leupold Mark 4 M1. These scopes are tremendously popular and often sold out. Because of their great expense ($810 each at press time), they are carried by relatively few dealers. Contact Leupold & Stevens, Inc., PO box 688, Beaverton, OR 97075-0688, to find out which dealers currently have these scopes in inventory.

Attaching 30mm scopes to a rattail Sako action has become incrementally easier and a bit more certain with advent of 30mm Leupold rings made especially for Sako actions. Medium—or more often high—mounts must be used to clear the tactical scope's huge objective lens.

Like country survivors, city types will quickly discover that sighting in a tactical rifle is a chore. City or country, there just ain't very many 1,000-yard ranges. To make matters worse, it is necessary to be able to drive between the shooting bench and the target. Using spotting scopes at 1,000 yards on relatively small, .30-caliber bullet holes, is a complete nonstarter.

After the rifle is sighted in, come-up cards can be developed listing exact scope settings for 350- , 450- , 600- , 800- , and 1,000-yard shots. Windage deflection is 4 inches per knot at 1,000 yards. Three-knot winds are common, which effectively put rounds outside most targets.

Practice-shooting these big, heavy rifles is enjoyable, but keep in mind that gilt-edge barrel life is only from 5,000 to 10,000 rounds!

Although vast experience and common sense suggest that shrewd city survivors looking for the best chance of survival should not get involved in combat actions around them, they should own at least one military-type semiauto assault rifle per family. Virtually any rifle will work in a pinch, but military designs are sturdier in long service, easier to repair, and, of course, use universal ammunition. Military .45-.70 rounds

Targets are so distant they cannot be seen without glasses. This range is 800 yards. Note the ribbon attached to the car's radio antenna indicating wind direction.

developed around 1872, for instance, are still popular in the United States!

Implementing this assault rifle acquisition philosophy is dramatically easier than it was 20 years ago. Currently dozens of firms manufacture all manner of parts sets, barrels, stocks, receiver types, and accessories for AR-15 type rifles. Personally I still prefer longer ranged, more powerful FN assault rifles in .308 NATO, but as a practical matter it's got to be an AR-15-type weapon, because FNs are pretty much unavailable.

In my lifetime I have encountered scores of guns—mostly pistols— that were about worthless because no magazine or too few magazines were available for them. Stock up on magazines and, of course, ammo. Ten high-capacity magazines per rifle plus 1,000 rounds of ammo is a figure experts frequently cite. At this level you will at least be "in the game" with sufficient firepower to appropriate additional weapons and ammunition, should this become expedient. With 10 extra mags, loss of one or even two will not be catastrophic.

THE RELIABLE .22

Successfully surviving in built-up areas is about deep hiding. City survivors must always keep their presence secret, which is often a difficult task when there are wild edibles to be taken or intruders to be quietly dealt with. As mentioned, this will require a good, familiar .22 rimfire rifle or a near equivalent and a silencer or a near equivalent.

Again, my dinosaurism may be showing, but I prefer a good old rugged .22 caliber bolt-action rifle to any other kind. Autos use too much ammo and seem more subject to malfunction. Levers and pumps are far too complicated in dirty, desperate circumstances. Keep in mind that .22s are for surreptitious duty, not primarily for defense, although there is that element as well. Slow reliable, long-lived bolts or even single-shots are OK.

SUBCALIBER DEVICES

Rifles set aside for duty around the retreat should be very quiet. Quietness can be accomplished with a silencer, low-velocity ammunition, subcaliber devices, or a combination of all of these. I prefer subcaliber devices, which currently are legal and can be just as quiet as illegal silencers. Many work well in existing rifles or

Quiet subcaliber devices are ideal when defending a city retreat area. Shown here are .300 Winchester Magnum, .308, and .32 ACP models.

Twelve-gauge shotgun inserts, having their own stubby barrels, accurately fire 9mm pistol and .223 rounds.

The author's favorite poaching combination: a .32 ACP in a .308 rifle. There is plenty of power to kill deer, the accuracy is good, and the noise level is low.

shotguns without modification. My .308/.32 ACP subcaliber device in a Remington Number Seven rifle will drill a phone book at 200 yards without changing the scope's setting!

Subcaliber devices are little gizmos that slip into standard rifles or shotguns, allowing them to fire smaller rifle or pistol ammunition. There are two types. One has its own short barrel, the other uses the barrel of the rifle in which it is operated.

I first encountered these devices in the Philippines on the Island of Mindanao in the hands of insurgents. They used a device allowing captured .223 or 9mm pistol ammo to be fairly accurately fired in 12- and 20-gauge shotguns. In this case, the device itself provided a short, rifled barrel that stabilized the bullets. They got about 9-inch groups at 150 to 200 meters—close enough for military work.

Subcaliber devices are made to convert a large number of rifle cartridges and calibers. In addition to ones allowing .223 and 9mm to be fired in a 12 gauge, I use models providing for .22 LRs to be fired in a .223; .32 ACP in a .308; and .22 LRs in a .30-06. Use of .32 ACPs in a .308 is very quiet. Virtually as quiet as conventional silenced rounds. Accuracy out of long guns is good to extremely good. We consistently place rounds in a 10-inch-square phone book at 200 yards with one of these devices. Fifteen years' experience indicates that, when shot in the head or neck at that range, deer-sized critters are efficiently reduced to possession.

During this era of suppression-fire philosophies, subcaliber devices are not particularly common or popular. Single-shot people like them, but to those who enjoy turning ammunition into a hail of fire, they are just a curiosity. Several national manufacturers produced these devices at one time. Currently MCA Sports and the Ace Bullet Co., 2800 West 33rd Road, Anchorage, AK 99517, are the only game in town. The price is about $25 each.

HANDGUNS

Nothing significant—except possibly the advent of supercompact carbines firing rifle rounds—has occurred that changes my mind regarding use of pistols in city survival situations. Truth is, most people do not use conventional pistols with sufficient skill to make them practical. Accuracy with a pistol at any range is really tough. True proficiency only comes by constant practice over a period of 6 to 8 years and, in my opinion, from being around someone who is a really good pistol shot. Apparently this association with an outstanding *pistolero* leads to personal confidence that one can really hit targets at extended ranges (more than 5 to 7 yards).

The display of a pistol on the belt leads to less crime and more civilized behavior; there's no question about that. But to say this is also true in a tough city survival situation is difficult.

But, assuming that getting hits on target with a sufficiently powerful single hand weapon to make a lasting impression is important, I would choose an AR-15 pistol with a 40-round magazine. Currently these either must be built from parts or from a kit offered by AR-15 component manufacturers. With a shorty stock they are marvelously effective weapons out to about 100 yards. Why they are not much more popular is a

With its double 40-round magazine, this AR-15 pistol is virtually a crew-served handgun. The firepower is tremendous, and hits on target count for something.

GUNS

Inexpensive to shoot and purchase, .22 Ruger handguns are probably best for survivors.

mystery. Probably because it is not easy to assemble one of these pistols and have it function reliably.

Yet, most city survivors will feel they must have some sort of handgun. This is understandable even if the idea is less than practically defensible. When funds are limited for both guns and ammo, it would seem wise to first lay in something common, reliable, and simple, such as a .22 LR. A rugged, reliable Ruger standard auto comes immediately to mind. Three important goals are accomplished. Owners of .22 handguns can learn to shoot at minimum cost and with minimum disruption. Also, they have a gun for which they should already have a ton of ammo.

Next, when it seems terribly important, I would purchase a high-quality, military-grade 9mm pistol. This will give you more options, because 9mm universal ammo is more likely purchased as surplus, scrounged, or captured. Military pistol designs are important because these guns have the ruggedness and reparability vital for city survivors.

My choice is still a high-capacity Browning Hi-Power or a Beretta Model 92. Certainly there are others just as good, but—like women—it's all in the eye of the beholder.

SHOTGUNS

No city survivor I talked with used shotguns of any type, in

Tactical shotguns have mostly disappeared from the American market. This SPAS 12 is complex and, in the author's opinion, of limited value for city survivors.

The Mossberg 500 shotgun is the most rugged model pump gun ever produced.

spite of the fact that shotguns are almost always the last guns to be demonized by governments. Perhaps this is because shotguns are so far removed from being military weapons. The fellow from Beirut simply said he wouldn't be able to get one because the military didn't use them.

Perhaps the military use of shotguns isn't widespread because they have limited range, make a great deal of noise, ammo is tough to resupply and cumbersome to carry in any quantity, and very few shotguns are of sufficient strength to stand up to military/survival duty. Under some specific circumstances, some shotguns may be acceptable military weapons in built-up areas, but keep in mind that we are going to keep our heads down and survive, not engage in military actions unless absolutely forced into it.

Word is that Mossberg 500 pumps are the most rugged, reliable shotguns ever built. These may be good weapons for those in cities. Mossberg 500s are also some of the least expensive weapons—but before embarking on this path, be sure sufficient funds are available for both a gun and a pile of ammo. Also understand that this weapon may never be put to good use by the survivor. Five hundred dollars will purchase the gun and 1,000 rounds of 12-gauge ammunition; but in this day and age, $500 may not be much of a problem, even if it is money spent with some inefficiency.

Other strictly military-type shotguns such as a SPAS 12, a Beretta 1201 FP, and the Benelli Black Eagle, have mostly disappeared from U.S. markets. Some of these shotguns were quite good, but some, like the SPAS 12, were far too complicated to be of great value. Military shotguns available today are prohibitively expensive, probably precluding purchase of more important sniper rifles, .22 rifles, assault rifles, and ammunition, except in the case of very well-heeled folks.

What do our been there, done that folks pick for guns? A longer range, optically sighted rifle, a simple .22 rifle with silencer or other quiet capability, an assault rifle, and an absolute trailerload of ammunition and magazines are all equally important, they claim.

But keep in mind that no foreigners, even those who have served in the military, know guns and ammo like Americans.

We can say absolutely that possession of personal firearms will be vital for survival. Few, if any, city survivors will make it without guns and lots of ammunition. No one can provide any evidence to the contrary. Does this also mean that antigun Easterners inhabiting one-third of the United States and most of the big built-up areas in our country are in for tough times in the future?

Better in this case to worry about ourselves, allowing whatever foolishness is being sown to establish itself at harvest.

Chapter 12

Survival Nursing

Nursing in a survival context seldom receives much interest and attention. Pity, since this single activity can save or—as more frequently occurs—lose significant numbers of lives. Especially when undertaken by uninformed, unprepared survivors.

Nursing in any form is defined as the act of providing skilled, appropriate, long-term sheltering care leading to successful convalescence and recovery from accidents, sickness, or wounds. Nursing for city survivors is especially critical because initial care provided by some persons who are less than skilled and trained may be borderline at best. In an emergency, we may be sewed up by nurses, dentists, pharmacists, farmers, veterinarians, dental assistants, chiropractors, and even at times common private citizens.

That all of these people are extremely well-intentioned and correspondingly anxious to do the right thing is little consolation. In a survival situation, even medical doctors will be constrained by a lack of proper drugs, instruments, and facilities. Placing an untrained or borderline amateur in these circumstances is definitely not ideal, but will be necessary if any lives are to be saved.

City survivors are also faced with the fact that because of the large number of people they may encounter in cities, they will also come across some who require long-term nursing care. We should understand that because of the nature of our existence, we will be called on to nurse many friends, family members, and close acquaintances found around us in cities who have also received less than ideal or even adequate initial care.

Standards of cleanliness were still primitive by today's standards, but during our own Civil War, it was received truth that patients quickly evacuated from central hospitals into private homes had the best chance of survival. Often it was not the shot-off legs or shattered ribs that killed patients, but rather horrible, raging, epidemic infections. Hospitals and central receiving areas for the wounded were notorious pest houses, which was intensified by the fact that no one in the medical profession knew what caused infections. In that regard alone, modern city survivors are at great advantage.

Patients allowed to remain even a few days at these central medical areas were virtually 100-percent certain of acquiring an infectious disease for which there was little hope. Two lines on the graph crossed creating this horror: the native strength of wounded men lying in bed ebbed while infections spread and raged.

Some knowledgeable folks still maintain that even today there is great risk of infection in our modern hospitals. Perhaps this is an overstatement, but only because rigorous measures are taken to minimize infectious conditions in hospitals. To a certain extent these measures are also available to city survivors.

Along with modern miracle disinfectants for both the patient and the room, modern hospitals have crews that do little but scrub, scrub, and scrub all day long. Even within the past 10 or 12 years, remarkable new technologies have come on the scene that give disease-causing germs less chance to hide and prosper. These include disease abatement, construction techniques, new and remarkable construction materials, special paints, sealers, and finishes that really keep dirt, filth, and infection in check and, of course, disinfectants that—by Civil War standards—are nothing short of miraculous.

One of the keys to survival nursing is getting your friend or loved one out of any central medical treatment area into a nursing

SURVIVAL NURSING

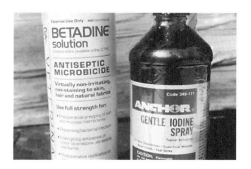

Antiseptics are miraculous in their application even when compared to materials available just 20 years ago.

retreat as quickly as possible. Then it is vital that the retreat *not* become a hospital. That is, treat this one patient or, at most a small batch of two or three patients, and then quit. Most nurses recommend waiting 3 or 4 months after the retreat is cleaned and disinfected before starting with the next batch of patients! The overlap of patients quickly leads to great concentrations of uncontrollable disease and infection.

City survivors have some dramatic modern disinfectants available to them. For patients themselves, we have Betadine, gentle iodine and hydrogen peroxide, among others. These materials are generally used to clean and treat personal wounds, but other especially good disinfectant materials useful on floors, walls, and ceilings are available from veterinary or farm supply stores. These are Bioguard X-185 containing 30 percent cresylic acid, Roccal D, 1 Stroke Environ, and even raw formaldehyde.

Because disinfecting barns and pig stalls is much tougher than disinfecting most bedrooms or tents, these materials are high powered, highly concentrated, state of the art, and extremely effective. They are certainly as good as anything in local hospitals.

Flies and lice may be a problem for survivors left too long in central receiving areas or in dirty, filthy retreats used by numbers of different people. At Stalingrad lice were epidemic among German soldiers. Lice just show up and prosper in those sorts of conditions. Again, some effective materials are available over the counter from your friendly vet supply store. These will give you the upper hand over flies and lice. Look for treatments with high concentrations of lindane and pyrethrins. These materials may also be used to help sterilize bedding, clothes, draperies, rugs, and tent bottoms. As a practical matter, survival nursing quarters should be on stone, cement, or finished wood. Avoid rugs or other porous materials.

Modern hospitals use mostly throwaway plastic kits for their procedures. Specialized kits, some of which are breathtakingly expensive, exist for virtually everything. They range from simple little packets designed to facilitate intravenous medications to great, elaborate affairs required for complete laparoscopic surgery. We won't have these pre-sterilized kits. Even if we did we couldn't afford to throw them out after just one use. Reportedly, some of these kits are presently recycled to some extent, but one wonders.

Commonly disposable items may be sterilized and reused in a survival situation.

Survival nurses will have to make provisions to sterilize all of their instruments that will be used repeatedly. Boil for at least 20 minutes all gear, including needles, hemostats, scalpels, and the like. In a survival context most of these tools are irreplaceable. All must be cleaned up and resterilized. In cases where boiling vigorously in a shallow, open container will either ruin the apparatus or may not clean and sterilize it, strong disinfectants can be used as a wash. Many times we do both. To an extent, infections are treatable with modern veterinary-grade antibiotics, but in a survival context these materials will be scarce. Why ask for additional trouble?

Likely we won't think of it now, but provision should be made to thoroughly incinerate bandages, cotton, infected clothes, bedding, and other miscellaneous contaminated items. Thorough burning will consume even more of our scarce energy supplies and could conceivably compromise our position, but it may be necessary to limit the chances of spreading disease.

Other disinfecting of bedding, clothes, and linens can be undertaken at the retreat in a kind of homemade, temporary autoclave. This device can be as simple as an old-fashioned covered cooker with a coarse rack in the bottom into which a pint of clean water is placed. When the water is boiled, steam penetrates upward into the clothes, doing a job on growies and little critters. Hopefully, it is obvious that clothes and bedding so treated are first thoroughly washed, using up yet more of our precious water supplies and time.

Place the covered container with cloth to be sterilized inside, over a gentle fire. Heat till the water is long gone, virtually scorching the clothes inside. During our Civil War, women working as nurses who were sufficiently fastidious to hot-iron all their laundry basically accomplished similar effects. Private people could do this work for individual patients, but on an areawide basis after a major battle it was unthinkable. Ironing clothes is easier today but not as widely done in our wash-and-wear society. At any rate, few clothes irons will be working after a collapse.

Good, sound shelters are necessary if our patients are to recover. These must be secure places that can be kept warm and dry, where meals can be provided and where waste disposal doesn't become an issue. Patients kept comfortable, without undue stress, for extended periods obviously are more likely to make it.

In cases of nursing situations, it may be necessary to pull way, way back, away from the conflict to a place of really deep seclusion. Great amounts of convenience, including accessibility to vital supplies, may need to be sacrificed for the sake of the patient and his recovery.

City survivors who take up nursing should also be aware that down through history this has been a very dangerous undertaking. Getting caught by the enemy is easier when mobility is sacrificed, and the penalty for getting caught is often summary execution. During our Civil War, the woman who did nothing more than rent a sleeping room to John Wilkes Booth was actually hanged by our military for her part in the assassination of Abraham Lincoln!

City survivors in general must engage in some pretty deep hiding. Those who also go into nursing will have to become absolutely paranoid. Witness the World War II Nazi treatment of Polish, Ukrainian, and Russian peasants who even thought about sheltering Jews.

ENERGY

Survival nursing will require prodigious quantities of energy for heating and hot water, Jackie, a nurse with long experience and now living in Chicago, told me. I asked what "prodigious" meant. She said it will take lots and lots of energy to heat water and the retreat, sterilize medical tools and bandages, cook food, and accomplish other tasks she couldn't presently think of to run any kind of a successful nursing program. Perhaps more than double what is needed for normal, day-to-day survival activities.

I then asked Betty Lou, who in the past 60 years has nursed scores of people back to health under incredibly primitive circumstances, about energy. "I buy wood from the people and I have 55-gallon barrels of kerosene delivered in, and of course any woman nurse should know how to run a chain saw."

"Run a chain saw?" I questioned.

"Yup, and here are the things women need to know," Betty Lou said. They sound practical for men as well. I repeat verbatim.

1. "Always use a Stihl-brand chain saw," she stated. "Others are

Nurses will use incredible amounts of fuel and may need to crank up their chain saws to make firewood.

too heavy, not sufficiently well made, and too hard to start. Women can't yank their shoulders out of joint pulling starter ropes on stupid, slow-starting chain saws, and they can't continually play around with petty maintenance," she continued.

A small, light Stihl model OV 28 is the most practical chain saw for women.

2. Use a smaller, lighter Stihl model OV 28 or thereabouts, weighing at most 7 to 9 pounds. Use at most a 20-inch bar (assembly on which the cutting chain runs). This will still cut through a 4-foot diameter tree, but won't pull smaller built women's arms out of joint during operations.
3. Pay great care to keeping the chain lubricated by refilling the chain lubrication reservoir with special oil at least every 30 minutes of operation. Women tend to forget this step. Chain oil is available from hardware or chain saw stores.
4. Never allow the chain to touch the ground, even when the saw is not running. A single, small nail in scrap lumber or a pebble can easily cause damage, requiring an hour of refiling the chain.
5. Learn to sharpen the chain and keep it very sharp.

This last item seemed like being told, "Win the lottery and live happily ever after." I asked Betty Lou to explain.

"Buy several chain saw files from the dealer of exactly the correct size," she explained. "These will probably be 7/32-inch size. Also, purchase a chain saw filer's guide, which holds the file high enough on the teeth so they are not hooked while providing guide marks so that the correct file angles are maintained.

"Tighten the chain on the bar so that it can be pulled up about half a tooth section on the guide bar and then begin to sharpen.

"File *only* from inside out, cutting only on the outstroke. Don't ever draw the file back across the tooth. Only push out. File one side completely and then turn the saw around to do all the teeth on the other side the same way."

Betty Lou pitches the file after six or eight uses. "My hands are not as strong as some men's hands. I don't like to keep using a dull, slow-cutting file," she says. She also cuts up lots of old building material, boards, beams, and wood siding. Often these have some small nails or screws. "Hit one and it's another 60 minutes resharpening the chain," she says. "These smaller, lighter, less powerful saws work poorly when their chains are dull," she says.

"Aren't there easier ways of securing energy?" I asked.

"Yes," she says, "but they are seldom convenient and survival nursing takes so much time and energy that we always have to be ready to use whatever is close at hand."

WATER

Water is another critical element of survival nursing. Great quantities of pure, wholesome water are required to hydrate patients, clean the retreat, and cook. Much of this must be hot water, suggesting yet another use for our already dwindling energy supplies.

Betty Lou developed a spring outside the city in which she usually works, but this technology is probably outside the scope of this book. But by whatever means, water supplies in a survival nursing situation must be dramatically expanded. It also calls for expansion of water-purifying systems.

It is best to plan for a bigger, better sand filtration rack, more bleach, and perhaps even some of the more expensive, faster acting water purification chemicals. Upping bleach use to 3 ounces per gallon, and/or allowing the mixture to sit 24 hours rather than 12 is workable. If survival nursing seems a possibility, lay in some 35-percent food-grade peroxide (which also stores relatively poorly). Have a supply of tetracycline hydroperiodide and titratable iodine tablets or even some plain old iodine tablets from your local pharmacy. Check local pharmacies, mail-order preparedness people, or backpack supply outlets for these chemicals. All are quite expensive, limiting use to nursing candidates.

Using one of the popular little 1-quart-per-minute 2-micron backpack filters is also a possibility. They range in price from $60 to about $150. From 200 to 300 gallons of water can be purified before another $50 filter must be installed. Most retreaters run their water through the sand filter first. Cost, speed, and service life usually limit these devices to producing water for patients.

NUTRITION

What is the most important nursing element for patients recovering from burns, breaks, and gunshot trauma?

Most people are surprised to discover it is nutrition. My first guess was a good supply of antibiotics. I was skeptical, so I asked several experts. I heard the same story time after time. When survival nursing is likely, lay in a huge supply of high-quality multiple vitamins and minerals, I was repeatedly told. Along with antibiotics, some of these are available from the vet supply counter.

Plan to feed quality meals, they said. A surgeon suggested that

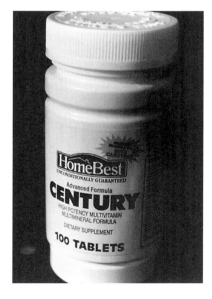

Good nutrition is a cornerstone of survival nursing.

The curative effects of chicken soup are no myth. Good nutrition does speed a cure.

I bone up on the five basic food groups. And they are not nicotine, caffeine, sugar, fat, and alcohol, he half-scolded with a twinkle in his eye.

Chicken soup's restorative powers are apparently no myth. Patients respond mightily to nutrition, adding yet another dimension to our storage needs and requirements. Basically, good nutrition depends on lots of clean water, fruit, fresh vegetables, meat, and grains daily. We are told to pay special attention that everything is prepared and served in the most sanitary manner possible. Improper food preparation can lead to a destruction of food value or, on the other end of the scale, to possible food poisoning.

We are to select one main course providing an adequate serving of meat. Bread or some sort of cereal should also be provided. Fruit and/or vegetables as available should be served at least once a day. Recovering patients may eat like hogs or they may eat like birds, including as many as five meals daily. A nurse's duty is to keep the patient clean, happy, and full of good, nutritious food. Not an altogether easy task, especially in primitive conditions. This simple-sounding philosophical concept is often about as important as storage, diagnosis, and then deployment of pharmaceutical drugs.

MEDICAL CONDITIONS

As mentioned in Chapter 10, initial care is a complex issue about which a bit has already been written. Those interested in medical matters not directly having to do with long-term nursing might look at *Survivalist's Medicine Chest* and *Do-It-Yourself Medicine*.

It is my firm conviction that survivors, including those in cities, are faced with three general categories of medical conditions. First of these are medical situations brought on by age, heredity, or general deterioration, over which we have little or no control and for which cures and effective treatments, in the hands of specialists, buy a few years at best.

Second are conditions directly caused by personal behavior which are completely avoidable. AIDS and lung cancer (for smokers) jump to mind as examples in this category. This is not to suggest that there are personal choices we should not make. Only that there are personal choices that all individuals must make knowing full well that the when they choose wrong, the consequences are severe.

Third are medical emergencies brought on by accidents, warfare, or environmental conditions that are definitely treatable by skilled, dedicated amateurs. These are the type of conditions where nursing is most effective. Obviously there is overlap. The challenge lies not in taking foolish, unrewarding risks, while still continuing at the same time to enjoy life to its fullest. Detonations and gunfire are an adrenaline rush for me, for instance. I already know I may not die in bed.

These last people who have consciously elected to get into the battle and are now hurt, who have contracted some awful disease or condition as a result of a filthy, unhealthy environment, or who have been abused by their fellow man are ones we can realistically expect to nurse back to life in our survival retreats.

I hope this brief introduction has sensitized all potential city survivors to the understanding that they will likely be faced with a survival nursing chore, what it will cost to undertake this chore, and how to proceed.

Conclusion

But will all of this stuff really work?

It's a fair question with which I am frequently confronted—principally by skeptical, nonpreparedness folks who really don't want it to work.

I'm thankful that most skeptics stay well outside the ranks of practicing survivalists. These skeptics are the types who fail to see any future need for any survival skills or knowledge. Planning ahead is the hallmark of the survivor. Obviously these are not plan-aheaders.

People who have actually lived through a collapsed- , fought-over, or abandoned-city survival scenario *all agree*—most of us can make it.

Significantly, most survivors never want to repeat the experience. "Even a pig," one especially devout Islamic Imam told me, "should not have to go through what I went through on our retreat from Delhi to Karachi." His confession after 50 years was so solidly sincere it was virtually tearful.

Being certain that some sort of collapse will likely occur in one of our big cities is necessary if one is to survive. Jews in Europe immediately prior to World War II were convinced that nothing worse could happen to them. Few made real, viable preparations.

"They just could not do all of the monstrous things Hitler,

Himmler, and Heydrich said they will do to us," was their plaintive cry. They are like some foolish, appeasing American gun owners today whose motto seems to be, "If we do just this one more stupid, ineffective thing, they will finally leave us alone."

When we were kids, we used to whistle as we walked past the cemetery at our property corner. How many wars, genocides, mass killings, and ethnic cleansings will it take before we realize that governments will never leave freedom-loving people alone?

All city survivors of any experience fervently wish they had taken the time and money to make more extensive prior preparations. It would have been much easier if they'd had a few more gallons of stored water, bags of flour, dollars to buy necessities, or whatever, they allsay.

Kosovo, Yugoslavia—this whole stinking mess has been constantly before me in the news as I worked on the manuscript for this book.

We heard it constantly on the news from reporters, government agents, apologists, and casual observers—these people were incapable of saving themselves, these naysayers claim. Fortunately, I was in constant contact with Ziga, a like-minded reader/informant in Slovenia whose considerable wisdom I share with readers. It is sufficient to understand that Slovenia is one of those bread slice-sized countries located in the region involved in the tumult.

Ziga makes several interesting points, the first of which may have little to nothing to do with city survival and perhaps little to do with survival in Kosovo.

"These Kosovars are the scariest gangsters!" Ziga writes. "They deal mostly with heroin, prostitution, and illegal, ruthless money-lending," he continues. "They cause a lot of trouble here." Like stereotyping any people, all this may be true or it may be that we tend to notice only the really rotten eggs in the basket.

Way back in 1991, very quickly after the Berlin Wall went down, Slobodan Milosevic sent his army to attack Slovenia. The Slovenian army, mostly militiamen, repulsed the attack in a matter of days. Slovenia has prospered economically in peace, even since. By European standards, excluding Switzerland, gun ownership in Slovenia is relatively easy, especially including black-market accessibility.

CONCLUSION

Perhaps as a face-saving technique, Milosevic immediately tried the same stunt in Croatia. These folks weren't so fortunate. They were forced to contend with both Milosevic's invading bullies and the NATO nations, through an arms embargo slapped on Croatia. In essence, we told the Croatians they were not allowed to defend themselves. This arms embargo on both the Croatians and the Kosovars ultimately subjected them to Yugoslavia's armies.

Ziga claims weapons up through Soviet RPGs and AK-47s are commonly available on the black market throughout the entire region. A full-auto AK-47, for instance, costs only 300 German marks (about U.S. $160 at current rates). As in the United States, black-market weapons won't keep tanks out of the petunia patch, but they will prevent military bullying on an individual basis.

On the other hand, to their utter destruction, residents of Kosovo actually believed that the government was somehow there to help them—that some force would show up to protect them from other government bullies. As history always demonstrates, people are not protected by their government. Historically, bullying is an official function of one's own government.

This explains the vital need for a solid emphasis on personal firearms within city survival situations. History is firmly on our side on this one. Only citizens, given the right and ability to fight back, will keep an evil man at the head of his evil army from doing more evil! We would have thought the world had learned this lesson from World War II.

But exactly how could residents of Kosovo have kept from becoming victim refugees? It's like a recap of this entire book.

They could have recognized early on that government can never guarantee safety—that at some point personal responsibility would always enter in.

After looking out at bitter experiences of others in nearby regions, they should have figured out that extensive preparations would be necessary. These preparations should have included provision for alternate shelter, food, water, defense, medical supplies, and whatever else their personal Rule of Threes suggested.

They should not have lived among potentially hostile people as identifiable targets. This would have entailed adopting plain vanilla dress as well as living and personal habits that kept them from standing out. Once hostilities became obvious, these folks would have had to engage in deep hiding.

Warsaw's Jews quickly discovered that by being forcibly collected together, they became an easy and perhaps popular target. On the other hand, the Nazis found that when Jews in the Warsaw Ghetto coalesced into fighting units, they became some pretty tough nuts! I am reliably informed that Albanians in Kosovo did nothing to help themselves. Their solution to the problem was to band together and run to another government for protection, not to band together to stand and fight.

Reliable accounts surface about the fact that Albanians in Kosovo were completely inflexible in their conduct of life. I asked Ziga whether it was true that "starving" Kosovars refused to eat U.S. Army field rations especially formulated for Islamic people. He said it was true.

These people consented to becoming refugees in spite of great world and regional evidence that refugees are frequently treated poorly.

They miserably failed to modify their religious practices when it became a life-and-death matter, and these practices were revealed to be more cultural than religious. Admittedly this is a touchy, difficult area, but I am assured by Islamic teachers that rape on the part of invading armies is not a religious death sentence for that society's Muslim women members, unless that society arbitrarily dictates that it is. As additional evidence, I was reminded of the great rape of the Muslim population in India at partition, and of the "de-oathing" of Mau Mau in Kenya to cite another religious example from Christianity. (In the case of Mau Mau, African individuals engaged in homosexual practices as part of their initiation ceremonies. It was supposed that these practices were so heinous that participants could never leave that society. However, a quasi-religious counter ceremony, known as de-oathing, was cobbled together, allowing Mau Maus to reform.)

At any rate, all of this suggests again that there is nothing out there that will keep us from making it through tough times in big cities. True enough, we will be laughed at, scorned, and made official pariahs for our preparedness beliefs and practices. That's the

CONCLUSION

way it is and that's the way it is going to be. We will also be the ones who build the next society. In that regard alone, we will have the last laugh.

About the Author

Ragnar Benson is the product of the last of the small 80-acre Midwestern subsistence farms. Currently he lives in the mountainous West but, because of advancing age, he has decreased the number of foreign "assignments" he will take on. He has lived and worked in 63 different countries.

Benson's current and past way of life reflects the survival philosophy he espouses. He actually lives the frugal, independent life of a survivor.

But Benson has spent a good deal of his life in the big city. Internationally he has had ample opportunity to see cause and effect of collapsed big-city economies. His father before him survived in post-World War I Germany and his mother was a survivor of the first Communist purges in Russia.

Ragnar is uncertain whether those skilled at city survival will have an easier or tougher time than their counterparts out in the country. The principles involved, but not the practices, are similar.

Both groups of survivors will have to work harder than they ever have in their lives, Benson speculates. His only concerns are that Americans have become too specialized and that they may lack motivation to actually survive in tough circumstances.

Having studied survival for well over 60 years, Benson is able to reduce the concept down to several easily understood guidelines. As with all of life, the devil is in the details. For varying reasons and for various lengths of time, city survivors are currently operating in different places around the world, Benson has found.

As much as anything, "A Hard-Times Guide to Staying Alive in the City" reflects how Benson currently lives.